HORNGREN'S ACCOUNTING

Tenth Canadian Edition
Volume 2

Tracie L. Miller-Nobles

Brenda Mattison

Ella Mae Matsumura

Carol A. Meissner

Jo-Ann L. Johnston

Peter R. Norwood

flex**Text**

PEARSON

Toronto

D1511639

Editorial Director: Claudine O'Donnell
Acquisitions Editor: Megan Farrell
Marketing Manager: Claire Varley
Program Manager: Karen Townsend
Project Manager: Pippa Kennard
Developmental Editor: Steven Lee
Composition: Cenveo® Publishing Services

Vice-President, Cross Media and Publishing Services: Gary Bennett

1 16

PEARSON

ISBN: 978-0-13-457655-8

Contents

Preface

Faculty

Welcome to Pearson's *flexText* for Horngren's Accounting 10th Canadian Edition. This student solution not only supports in-class work, but is also one of the many tools that Pearson has published to support various teaching strategies.

The *flexText* facilitates the flipped classroom approach to course delivery, where you might spend a portion of class time having students work either individually or in groups on guided problems. If a fully flipped class isn't your goal, but you still want to give students time in class to work on guided problem-solving exercises, this tool can be used to achieve that as well.

Students

Here is another tool to add to your toolkit for success. Read the full e-text and practice some questions online. Then in the classroom, get a near-to-real-world experience of using pencil and paper to prepare for tests.

Remember, the key to success in learning any new task is practice, practice, practice. The *flexText* will help you do this more efficiently because the questions are shown right where you work on the answers. It also keeps your work all neat and organized because the working papers are already formatted and ordered for you.

Pearson *flexText*: A Key for Success in School and at Work

Regardless of the course you're taking—whether you are in General Business, Marketing, Entrepreneurship, Accounting, Human Resources, or any other program—you will want to leave with skills that can help you get the job you want. Some of these skills will be specific to your course of study or major. These are basic skills your employers will want you to have. An accountant, for example, will be expected to know how to read a balance sheet and write journal entries. However, there are other skills essential to your success in the workplace that might not seem so obvious but are important enough that some governments call them "Essential" Employability Skills. The Conference Board of Canada goes even further, calling them "the skills you need to enter, stay in, and progress in the world of work—whether you work on your own or as a part of a team." (http://www.conferenceboard.ca/topics/education/learning-tools/employability-skills.aspx)

This Pearson *flexText* was designed to help you develop these skills.

What are Essential Employability Skills?

Essential Employability Skills can be grouped into six broad categories: Communication, Numeracy, Critical Thinking & Problem Solving, Information Management, Interpersonal, and Personal. The government of Ontario thinks that these skills are so important that they expect everyone who graduates with a certificate or diploma to have them. Other provincial governments place an equal emphasis on them as well. Many of these skills are also referred to as "soft skills," or "21st century skills," and represent areas like writing that are not specific to the core content of any one course but are important to your success in *all* courses, and in the working world. Being able to show prospective employers that you have these skills can make a huge difference in your ability to get the job that you want.

Pearson's *flexText* is designed with the needs of college students in mind, including the need to develop and demonstrate Essential Employability Skills. Here's how.

COMMUNICATION SKILLS

Defining skill areas: reading, writing, speaking, listening, presenting, and visual literacy

One of the reasons why students don't develop their reading skills is simply because they have not bought their textbooks at all. *flexTexts* are affordable, and available at a price that will encourage as many students as possible to buy—and read—their course materials. *flexTexts* often include short answer questions or writing activities that provide opportunities for students to practice and develop their written communication skills.

NUMERACY SKILLS

Defining skill areas: understanding and applying mathematical concepts and reasoning, analyzing and using mathematical data, and conceptualizing

flexTexts in disciplines such as Accounting require students to understand and apply some mathematical concepts when answering practice questions. The spiral bound *flexText* format encourages their use as in-class activity workbooks, where faculty can provide instructional support to students as they work through these problems.

CRITICAL THINKING & PROBLEM SOLVING SKILLS

Defining skill areas: analyzing, synthesizing, evaluating, decision making, and creative and innovative thinking

The exercises and activities found in Pearson's *flexTexts* are not simply factual, recall, or "skill and drill" type activities. They are created to engage students at many different levels of Bloom's Taxonomy to help develop their critical thinking and problem solving skills. And because the *flexText* is affordable, a greater number of students can purchase their course materials, gaining the opportunity to develop these skills through practice.

INFORMATION MANAGEMENT SKILLS

Defining skill areas: gathering and managing information, selecting and using appropriate tools and technology for a task or project, computer literacy, and internet skills

Not all of the exercises in a *flexText* are pencil and paper activities. Some also require students to engage with applications such as Microsoft Excel, or to explain how they would utilize these tools to find the solution to a problem.

INTERPERSONAL SKILLS

Defining skill areas: teamwork, relationship management, conflict resolution, leadership, and networking

Because *flexTexts* are designed to be used in class, they facilitate group work and collaborative problem solving. Activities that, in the past, would have been assigned as homework to be done individually can now be implemented in ways that help students develop their interpersonal skills.

PERSONAL SKILLS

Defining skill areas: managing self, managing change and being flexible and adaptable, engaging in reflexive practice, and demonstrating personal responsibility

Making the decision to purchase course materials and actively engage with course content is one of the first steps towards demonstrating a degree of personal responsibility for success in school. The page layout of a *flexText* also encourages note-taking and supports the development of good study skills.

12 PARTNERSHIPS

LEARNING OBJECTIVES

1 Identify the characteristics of a partnership.
2 Account for partners' initial investments in a partnership.
3 Allocate profits and losses to the partners by different methods.
4 Account for the admission of a new partner.
5 Account for the withdrawal of a partner.
6 Account for the liquidation of a partnership.

Starter 12–1 ①

For each of the three independent situations below, indicate if you would recommend the partnership form of business organization. State the reasons for your recommendation.

1. Sarah, Alisha, and Connie just graduated from a two-year college program and would like to start a bookkeeping business called SAC Bookkeeping. They each have equivalent assets to bring to the business.

2. Philip Harcourt just joined the law practice of Osler and Hoskins. He thinks he will be making a huge salary and is worried about the tax effects of this income. He thinks the partners should incorporate the partnership and avoid the tax bill.

3. Fred Klaus and Felix Cadeau would like to form a construction company. Fred has the contacts, cash, and estimating skills, while Felix has equipment and field experience. There will be minimal profits until the business has a few projects.

Requirements 1 – 3

_____

_____

_____

_____

_____

_____

_____

_____

_____

_____

_____

_____

_____

_____

_____

_____

_____

_____

_____

_____

_____

Starter 12–4 ②

On June 30, 2016, Rick Reeves, Jason Bateman, and Oliver Morali started a partnership called RJO Enterprises. Prepare an opening balance sheet showing their investments:

R. Reeves	Land appraised at $150,000
J. Bateman	Cash, $175,000
O. Morali	Inventory, $105,000; accounts payable $30,000

Starter 12–5 ③

Abel and Baker decided to form a partnership. Abel contributed equipment (book value $65,000), inventory (paid $20,000), and $10,000 cash. The equipment and inventory have a current market value of $40,000 and $15,000, respectively. Abel also had a debt of $20,000 for the equipment. Baker contributed office equipment (book value $20,000) and cash of $50,000. The current market value of the office equipment is $10,000. The two partners fail to agree on a profit-and-loss-sharing ratio. For the first month (June 2017), the partnership lost $4,000.

1. How much of this loss goes to Abel? How much goes to Baker?

2. The partners withdrew no assets during June. What is each partner's Capital balance at June 30? Prepare a T-account for each partner's Capital.

Requirement 1

_____
_____
_____
_____
_____
_____
_____
_____
_____
_____

Requirement 2

Starter 12–6 ③

Friesen, Walters, and Onley have Capital balances of $12,000, $6,000, and $6,000, respectively. The partners share profits and losses as follows:

a. The first $40,000 is divided based on the partners' capital investments.

b. The next $30,000 is based on service, shared equally by Friesen and Onley.

c. The remainder is divided equally.

Compute each partner's share of the $94,000 net income for the year.

Requirements a. – c.

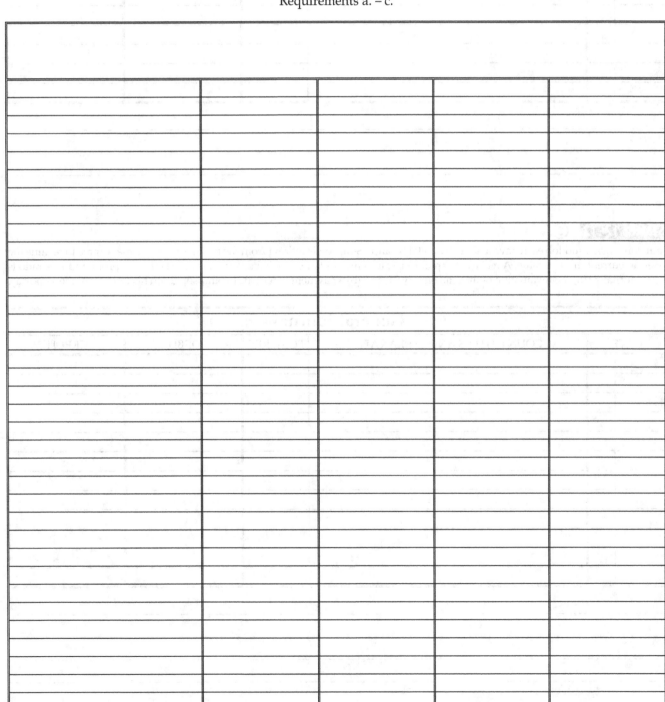

Starter 12–8 ④

Todd has a Capital balance of $60,000; Carlson's balance is $50,000. Reynaldo pays $200,000 to purchase Carlson's interest in the Todd & Carlson partnership. Carlson gets the full $200,000.

Journalize the partnership's transaction to admit Reynaldo to the partnership on August 1.

General Journal

DATE	ACCOUNT TITLES AND EXPLANATIONS	POST. REF.	DEBIT	CREDIT

Starter 12–12 ⑤

Simpson, Locke, and Job each have a $27,000 Capital balance. Simpson is retiring from the business. The partners agree to revalue the assets at current market value. A real estate appraiser values the land at $70,000 (book value is $50,000). The profit-and-loss ratio is 1:2:1. Journalize (a) the revaluation of the land on July 31, and (b) a payment of $32,000 to Simpson upon his retirement the same day.

General Journal

DATE	ACCOUNT TITLES AND EXPLANATIONS	POST. REF.	DEBIT	CREDIT

Starter 12–13 ⑥

Suppose the partnership of Lauren, Andrews, and Benroudi liquidates by selling all noncash assets for $80,000. Complete the liquidation schedule as shown in Exhibit 12–6.

	Cash	+	Noncash Assets	+	Liabilities	Capital Lauren (60%)	+	Andrews (20%)	+	Benroudi (20%)
Balance before sale of assets	$10,000		$90,000		$30,000	$40,000		$20,000		$10,000
1. Sale of assets and sharing of loss										
Balances										
2. Payment of liabilities										
Balances										
3. Disbursement of cash to partners										
Balances										

_____

_____

_____

_____

_____

_____

_____

_____

_____

Exercise 12–1 ①

Mark Giltrow and Denise Chan are forming a business to imprint T-shirts. Giltrow suggests that they organize as a partnership to avoid the unlimited liability of a proprietorship. According to Giltrow, partnerships are not very risky.

Giltrow explains to Chan that if the business does not succeed, each partner can withdraw from the business, taking the same assets that she or he invested at its beginning. Giltrow states that the main disadvantage of the partnership form of organization is double taxation: First, the partnership pays a business income tax; second, each partner also pays personal income tax on her or his share of the business's profits.

Correct the errors in Giltrow's explanation.

_____

_____

_____

_____

_____

_____

_____

_____

_____

_____

_____

_____

_____

_____

_____

_____

_____

_____

_____

Exercise 12–3 ②

Jackson Cooke and Julia Bamber are forming a partnership to develop an amusement park near Ottawa. Cooke contributes cash of $3 million and land valued at $30 million. When Cooke purchased the land, its cost was $16 million. The partnership will assume Cooke's $6 million note payable on the land. Bamber invests cash of $15 million and construction equipment that she purchased for $14 million (accumulated amortization to date is $6 million). The equipment's market value is equal to its book value.

Required

1. Journalize the partnership's receipt of assets and liabilities from Cooke and Bamber on November 10. Record each asset at its current market value with no entry to accumulated amortization.

2. Compute the partnership's total assets, total liabilities, and total owners' equity immediately after organizing.

Requirements 1 & 2

		General Journal			
DATE		ACCOUNT TITLES AND EXPLANATIONS	POST. REF.	DEBIT	CREDIT

_____

_____

_____

_____

_____

Exercise 12–4 ②

On January 1, 2016, Chris Hunts and Carol Lo formed the Chris and Carol Partnership by investing the following assets and liabilities in the business:

	Chris's Book value	Carol's Book value
Cash	$12,000	$18,500
Equipment	38,000	53,500
Accumulated amort.—equipment	8,200	9,900
Buildings	84,000	95,000
Accumulated amort.—buildings	25,000	35,000
Land	60,000	66,000
Accounts payable	35,000	35,000
Note payable	17,000	28,000

An independent appraiser believes that Chris's equipment has a market value of $29,000 and Carol's equipment has a market value of $47,500. The appraiser indicates Chris's building has a current value of $90,000 and Carol's building has a current value of $110,000. The appraiser further indicates that Chris's land has a current value of $78,000 and Carol's land has a current value of $80,000. Chris and Carol agree to share profits and losses in a 60:40 ratio. During the first year of operations, the business net income is $74,000. Each partner withdrew $30,000 cash.

Required

1. Prepare the journal entries to record the initial investments in the business by Chris and Carol.
2. Prepare a balance sheet dated January 1, 2016, after the completion of the initial journal entries.

Requirement 1

General Journal

DATE		ACCOUNT TITLES AND EXPLANATIONS	POST. REF.	DEBIT	CREDIT

Requirement 2

Exercise 12–5   ③

Ken Danolo and Jim Goldman form a partnership, investing $96,000 and $168,000, respectively. Determine their shares of net income or net loss for each of the following situations:

a. Net loss is $124,800 and the partners have no written partnership agreement.

b. Net income is $105,600 and the partnership agreement states that the partners share profits and losses based on their capital investments.

c. Net income is $264,000. The first $132,000 is shared based on the partner's capital investments. The next $100,000 is shared based on partner service, with Danolo receiving 40 percent and Goldman receiving 60 percent. The remainder is shared equally.

a. – c.

Exercise 12–6   ③

Harper, Cheves, and Calderon have capital investments of $20,000, $30,000, and $50,000, respectively. The partners share profits and losses as follows:

a. The first $40,000 is divided based on the partner's capital investments.

b. The next $40,000 is based on service, shared equally by Harper and Cheves.

c. The remainder is divided equally.

Compute each partner's share of the $92,000 net income for the year.

Exercise 12–7 ③

Oscar and Elmo have formed a partnership and invested $50,000 and $70,000, respectively. They have agreed to share profits as follows:

a. Oscar is to receive a payment of $25,000 for his service and Elmo is to receive a payment of $15,000 for his service.

b. $12,000 is to be allocated according to their original capital contributions to the partnership.

c. The remainder is to be allocated 5:4 respectively.

Assuming that the business had a loss of $11,000, allocate the loss to Oscar and Elmo.

Exercise 12–9 ④

Goertz Accounting Services has a capital balance of $30,000 after adjusting assets to the fair market value. Leonard Goertz wants to form a partnership with Morley Neilson, who will receive a 30 percent interest in the new partnership. Neilson contributes $17,000 for his 30 percent interest. Determine Neilson's equity after admission and any bonus if applicable.

Exercise 12–17   ②

Michael Lee has been running Lee Management Consulting as a proprietorship but is planning to expand operations in the near future. The revised Lee Management Consulting July 31, 2016, balance sheet appears on the next page, with all amounts adjusted to current market values so they can be used for the start of a partnership. Michael Lee is considering forming a partnership with Jill Monroe, who provides the market value financial information shown on the next page. Create the Lee and Monroe Consulting partnership balance sheet at July 31, 2016, assuming there are no payables or receivables between Lee and Monroe.

	Lee Management Consulting	Monroe's Business
Assets		
Cash	$21,650	$100,000
Accounts receivable	5,900	50,000
Inventory	2,713	5,000
Supplies	100	1,000
Prepaid rent	6,000	0
Equipment	1,000	10,000
Accumulated amortization—equipment	(75)	(100)
Furniture	5,000	4,000
Accumulated amortization—furniture	(267)	(900)
Total assets	$42,021	$169,000
Liabilities and Equity		
Accounts payable	$9,600	$ 20,000
Salary payable	1,000	0
Unearned service revenue	1,200	0
Notes payable	0	50,000
Michael Lee, capital	30,221	—
Jill Monroe, capital	—	99,000
Total liabilities and equity	$42,021	$169,000

Problem 12–1A ②

Vince Sharma and Klaus Warsteiner formed a partnership on January 1, 2017. The partners agreed to invest equal amounts of capital. Sharma invested his proprietorship's assets and liabilities (all accounts have normal balances):

	Sharma's Book Value	Current Market Value
Accounts receivable..	$24,000	$20,000
Inventory...	86,000	62,000
Prepaid expenses..	13,000	12,000
Store equipment..	72,000	52,000
Accounts payable..	40,000	40,000

On January 1, Warsteiner invested cash in an amount equal to the current market value of Sharma's partnership capital. The partners decided that Sharma would earn 70 percent of partnership profits because he would manage the business. Warsteiner agreed to accept 30 percent of profits. During the period ended December 31, 2017, the partnership earned $432,000. Warsteiner's withdrawals were $128,000 and Sharma's withdrawals were $172,800.

Required

1. Journalize the partners' initial investments.
2. Prepare the partnership balance sheet immediately after its formation on January 1, 2017.
3. Calculate the partners' Capital balances on December 31, 2017.

Requirement 1

General Journal

DATE	ACCOUNT TITLES AND EXPLANATIONS	POST. REF.	DEBIT	CREDIT

Requirement 2

Requirement 3

Students may EITHER complete a statement of partners' equity (see Exhibit 12-3) OR use T-accounts to calculate the capital account balances.

	SHARMA	WARSTEINER	TOTAL

Requirement 3 (Continued)

Problem 12–2A ③

Sheila Sasso, Karen Schwimmer, and Jim Perry have formed a partnership. Sasso invested $60,000, Schwimmer $120,000, and Perry $180,000. Sasso will manage the store, Schwimmer will work in the store three-quarters of the time, and Perry will not work in the business.

Required

1. Compute the partners' shares of profits and losses under each of the following plans:

   a. Net loss is $70,500, and the partnership agreement allocates 45 percent of profits to Sasso, 35 percent to Schwimmer, and 20 percent to Perry. The agreement does not discuss the sharing of losses.

   b. Net income for the year is $136,500. The first $45,000 is allocated on the basis of partners' Capital investments. The next $75,000 is based on service, with $45,000 going to Sasso and $30,000 going to Schwimmer. Any remainder is shared equally.

   c. Net loss for the year is $136,500. The first $45,000 is allocated on the basis of partners' Capital investments. The next $75,000 is based on service, with $45,000 going to Sasso and $30,000 going to Schwimmer. Any remainder is shared equally.

2. Revenues for the year were $858,000 and expenses were $721,500. Under plan (b), prepare the partnership income statement for the year. Assume a year end of September 30, 2017.

3. How will what you have learned in this problem help you manage a partnership?

Requirement 1 (Plan a)

	SASSO	PERRY	SCHWIMMER	TOTAL

Requirement 1 (Plan b)

	SASSO	PERRY	SCHWIMMER	TOTAL

Requirement 1 (Plan c)

	SASSO	PERRY	SCHWIMMER	TOTAL

Requirement 2

Requirement 3

Problem 12–4A ④

Sudden Valley Resort is a partnership, and its owners are considering admitting Ben Peller as a new partner. On July 31, 2017, the Capital accounts of the three existing partners and their shares of profits and losses are as follows:

	Capital	Profit-and-Loss Percentage
Eleanor Craven......................	$20,000	20%
Amy Osler............................	30,000	30
Brian Harmon.......................	40,000	50

Required Journalize the admission of Peller as a partner on July 31, 2017, for each of the following independent situations:

a. Peller pays Harmon $55,000 cash to purchase Harmon's interest.

b. Peller invests $30,000 in the partnership, acquiring a one-quarter interest in the business.

c. Peller invests $30,000 in the partnership, acquiring a one-sixth interest in the business.

Requirement a

	General Journal			
DATE	ACCOUNT TITLES AND EXPLANATIONS	POST. REF.	DEBIT	CREDIT

Requirement b

	General Journal			
DATE	ACCOUNT TITLES AND EXPLANATIONS	POST. REF.	DEBIT	CREDIT

Requirement c

General Journal

DATE		ACCOUNT TITLES AND EXPLANATIONS	POST. REF.	DEBIT	CREDIT

Problem 12–6A   ⑥

The partnership of Malkin, Neale, & Staal has experienced operating losses for three consecutive years. The partners, who have shared profits and losses in the ratio of Lisa Malkin, 20 percent, John Neale, 40 percent, and Brian Staal, 40 percent, are considering liquidating the business. They ask you to analyze the effects of liquidation under various assumptions about the sale of the noncash assets. They present the following partnership balance sheet amounts at December 31, 2017:

Cash	$ 41,000	Liabilities	$151,000
Noncash assets	367,000	Lisa Malkin, capital	57,500
		John Neale, capital	158,500
		Brian Staal, capital	41,000
Total assets	$408,000	Total liabilities and capital	$408,000

Required

1. Prepare a summary of liquidation transactions (as illustrated in the chapter) for each of the following situations:
   a. The noncash assets are sold for $420,000.
   b. The noncash assets are sold for $338,000.
2. Make the journal entries to record the liquidation transactions in Requirement 1(b).

Requirement 1a

Calculations:

Requirement 1b

Calculations:

Requirement 2

General Journal

DATE		ACCOUNT TITLES AND EXPLANATIONS	POST. REF.	DEBIT	CREDIT

Problem 12–8A ② ③ ④ ⑤

2014

Jun. 10 Adam Buckner and Amber Kwan have agreed to pool their assets and form a partnership to be called B&K Consulting. They agree to share all profits equally and make the following initial investments:

	Buckner	Kwan
Cash...	$15,000	$30,000
Accounts receivable (net)................	33,000	27,000
Office furniture................................	36,000	24,000

Dec. 31 The partnership's reported net income was $195,000 for the year ended December 31, 2014.

2015

Jan. 1 Buckner and Kwan agree to accept Heidi Nguen into the partnership with a $180,000 investment for 30 percent of the business. The partnership agreement is amended to provide for the following sharing of profits and losses:

	Buckner	Kwan	Nguen
Service..	$90,000	$120,000	$75,000
Interest on capital balance.................	5%	5%	5%
Balance in ratio of..............................	3 :	2 :	5

Dec. 31 The partnership's reported net income was $480,000.

2016

Oct. 10 Buckner withdrew $84,000 cash from the partnership and Kwan withdrew $57,000 (Nguen did not make any withdrawals).

Dec. 31 The partnership's reported net income was $255,000.

2017

Jan. 2 After a disagreement as to the direction in which the partnership should be moving, Nguen decided to withdraw from the partnership. The three partners agreed that Nguen could take cash of $300,000 in exchange for her equity in the partnership.

Required

1. Journalize all of the transactions for the partnership.

2. Prepare the partners' equity section of the B&K Consulting balance sheet as of January 2, 2017.

To track account balances

DATE		DESCRIPTION	BUCKNER	KWAN	NGUEN	TRANSACTION TOTAL

Requirement 1

General Journal

DATE		ACCOUNT TITLES AND EXPLANATIONS	POST. REF.	DEBIT	CREDIT

Requirement 1 (Continued)

		General Journal			
DATE		ACCOUNT TITLES AND EXPLANATIONS	POST. REF.	DEBIT	CREDIT

Requirement 2

13 CORPORATIONS: SHARE CAPITAL AND THE BALANCE SHEET

LEARNING OBJECTIVES

1 Identify the characteristics of a corporation.
2 Record the issuance of shares and prepare the shareholders' equity section of a corporation's balance sheet.
3 Account for cash dividends.
4 Use different share values in decision making.
5 Evaluate a company's ROA and ROE.
6 Identify the impact of IFRS on share capital.

Starter 13–2 ①

How does a proprietorship's balance sheet differ from a corporation's balance sheet? How are the two balance sheets similar?

_____

_____

_____

_____

_____

_____

_____

_____

_____

_____

_____

_____

_____

_____

_____

_____

_____

Starter 13-6 ②

Hatteras Corporation reported the following accounts (a partial list):

Cost of Goods Sold	$29,400	Accounts Payable	$ 3,000
Common Shares,		Retained Earnings	8,000
40,000 shares issued and outstanding	29,500	Unearned Revenue	2,600
Long-term Note Payable	3,800	Cash	12,000
Total assets	?		

Prepare the shareholders' equity section of the Hatteras balance sheet.

Starter 13–10 ③

Xiong Inc. has the following shareholders' equity:

Preferred shares, $0.025, cumulative, liquidation value $0.50, 50,000 shares authorized, 45,000 shares issued and outstanding	$ 20,000
Common shares, 1,000,000 shares authorized and issued and outstanding	200,000
Retained earnings	130,000
Total shareholders' equity	$350,000

Answer these questions about Xiong's dividends:

1. Are Xiong Inc.'s preferred shares cumulative or noncumulative? How can you tell?

2. Suppose Xiong Inc. declares cash dividends of $17,000 for 2017. How much of the dividends goes to preferred shares? How much goes to common shares?

3. Suppose Xiong Inc. did not pay the preferred dividend in 2015 and 2016. In 2017, the company declares cash dividends of $17,000. How much of the dividends goes to preferred shares? How much goes to common shares?

Requirements 1 – 3

Starter 13–12 ④

Midnight Distribution Corporation's balance sheet reported the following information at December 31, 2016:

Preferred shares, $3, cumulative, 11,000 shares issued, liquidation value $55 per share	$ 605,000
Common shares, 75,000 shares issued	2,000,000
Total contributed capital	2,605,000
Retained earnings	1,950,000
Total shareholders' equity	$4,555,000

Assuming there are two years' dividends in arrears (including 2016), determine the book value per share of both preferred and common shares.

Book value per
preferred share:

Book value per
common share:

Starter 13–13 ⑤

Township Corp.'s 2017 financial statements reported the following items—with 2016 figures given for comparison:

Balance sheet	2017	2016
Total assets	$49,000	$44,800
Total liabilities	$25,400	$22,000
Total shareholders' equity (all common)	23,600	22,800
Total liabilities and equity	$49,000	$44,800

Income statement	
Net sales	$39,130
Cost of goods sold	14,210
Gross margin	24,920
Selling and administrative expenses	14,000
Interest expense	400
All other expenses, net	4,420
Net income	$ 6,100

Compute Township Corp.'s rate of return on total assets and rate of return on common shareholders' equity for 2017. Do these rates of return look high or low?

Rate of return
on total assets:

Rate of return
on common
shareholders' equity:

Exercise 13–3 ①

Boogz Corp.'s new accounting intern prepared their adjusted trial balance in alphabetical order. All accounts have their normal balances.

Accounts Receivable	$ 56,000	Other Expenses	$ 35,400
Accumulated Amortization	14,000	Retained Earnings	68,400
Amortization Expense	40,800	Salaries Expense	170,000
Cash	112,000	Salaries Payable	3,400
Common Shares	50,000	Service Revenue	356,400
Computers & Equipment	74,800	Supplies	5,600
Interest Expense	8,800	Unearned Revenues	5,400
Interest Revenue	5,800		

Required

1. Prepare the appropriate closing entries for the January 31 year end.
2. What is the balance in the Retained Earnings account after the closing entries have been completed?

Requirement 1

General Journal

DATE	ACCOUNT TITLES AND EXPLANATIONS	POST. REF.	DEBIT	CREDIT

Requirement 2

Retained Earnings

Exercise 13–5 ②

Atul Incorporated made the following share issuance transactions:

Jan.   19   Issued 4,500 common shares for cash of $11.00 per share.

Feb.   3   Sold 1,000 $1.50 Class A preferred shares for $14,000 cash.

      11   Received inventory valued at $20,000 and equipment with market value of $17,000 for 5,800 common shares.

      15   Issued 2,000 $1.00 Class B preferred shares for $13.00 per share.

Required

1. Journalize the transactions. Explanations are not required.

2. How much contributed capital did these transactions generate for Atul Incorporated?

Requirement 1

General Journal

DATE		ACCOUNT TITLES AND EXPLANATIONS	POST. REF.	DEBIT	CREDIT

Requirement 2

Exercise 13–6 ②

Shapalov Supplies Ltd. imports farm equipment. The corporation issues 10,000 common shares for $15.00 per share. Record issuance of the shares on March 4.

General Journal

DATE	ACCOUNT TITLES AND EXPLANATIONS	POST. REF.	DEBIT	CREDIT

Exercise 13–7 ②

Sutherland Equipment Ltd. has a choice about how it records the acquisition of property, plant, and equipment in return for shares. Make the journal entries on February 5 for each of the following cases:

Case A—Issue shares and buy the assets in separate transactions:

Sutherland Equipment Ltd. issued 7,000 common shares for cash of $1,460,000. In a separate transaction, Sutherland then used the cash to purchase an office building for $900,000 and equipment for $560,000. Journalize the two transactions.

Case B—Issue shares to acquire the assets:

Sutherland Equipment Ltd. issued 7,000 common shares to acquire an office building valued at $900,000 and equipment worth $560,000. Journalize this transaction.

Compare the balances in all accounts in Case A and Case B. Are the account balances similar or different?

Case A

General Journal

DATE	ACCOUNT TITLES AND EXPLANATIONS	POST. REF.	DEBIT	CREDIT

Case B

General Journal

DATE		ACCOUNT TITLES AND EXPLANATIONS	POST. REF.	DEBIT	CREDIT

_____

_____

_____

_____

_____

_____

Exercise 13–8 ②

The articles of incorporation for Mid-way Consulting Inc. authorize the company to issue 500,000 $5 preferred shares and 1,000,000 common shares. During its first year of operations, Mid-way Consulting Inc. completed the following selected transactions:

2017

Jan.   4   Issued 5,000 common shares to the consultants who formed the corporation, receiving cash of $140,000.

      13   Issued 500 preferred shares for cash of $55,000.

      14   Issued 4,000 common shares in exchange for land valued at $120,000.

Dec. 31   Earned a profit for the fiscal year and closed the $150,000 net income into Retained Earnings.

Required

1. Record the transactions in the general journal.
2. Prepare the shareholders' equity section of the Mid-way Consulting Inc. balance sheet at December 31, 2017.

Requirement 1

| \multicolumn{6}{c}{**General Journal**} | | | | | |
DATE		ACCOUNT TITLES AND EXPLANATIONS	POST. REF.	DEBIT	CREDIT

Requirement 2

Exercise 13–10 ②

The articles of incorporation for Novak Technology Inc. authorize the issuance of 100,000 preferred shares and 250,000 common shares. During a two-month period, Novak Technology Inc. completed these share-issuance transactions:

Mar. 23   Issued 12,000 common shares for cash of $10.00 per share.

Apr. 12   Received inventory valued at $60,000 and equipment with a market value of $10,000 for 5,000 common shares.

17   Issued 1,500 $2.25 preferred shares. The issue price was cash of $11.00 per share.

Required

1. Journalize the transactions, with explanations.
2. Prepare the shareholders' equity section of the Novak Technology Inc. balance sheet for the transactions given in this exercise. Retained Earnings has a balance of $65,000.

Requirement 1

General Journal

DATE		ACCOUNT TITLES AND EXPLANATIONS	POST. REF.	DEBIT	CREDIT

Requirement 2

Exercise 13–12 ②

The following is an alphabetical list of accounts of CHFI Services Inc. as at January 31, 2016. The balances are *prior* to the closing journal entries. All accounts have normal balances.

Accrued Liabilities	$ 50,400
Accounts Payable	90,000
Accounts Receivable, net	318,000
Cash	494,000
Common Shares, 500,000 shares authorized; 200,000 shares issued	2,500,000
Interest Expense	29,000
Inventory	420,000
Long-term Note Payable	600,000
Organization Costs	18,000
Prepaid Expenses	3,600
Preferred Shares, $2.50, cumulative, 24,000 authorized and issued	240,000
Property, Plant, and Equipment, net	3,360,000
Retained Earnings	623,600
Trademark, net	20,400

Additional information:

Net income for 2016 was $530,000.

No new shares were issued in 2016.

Required Prepare a classified balance sheet as at January 31, 2016.

Exercise 13–13 ③

Melbourne Incorporated has 75,000 shares of $2 cumulative preferred shares outstanding as well as 110,000 common shares. There are no dividends in arrears on the preferred shares. The following transactions were reported during November 2016:

Nov. 1 Declared the required dividend on the preferred shares and a $0.23 per share dividend on the common shares.

14 The date of record for the dividend declared on November 1.

28 Paid the dividend declared on November 1.

30 Closed out the Income Summary account. Net income for the year was $257,000.

Required

1. Prepare journal entries to record the above transactions. No explanations are required.
2. Assuming the balance of Retained Earnings on December 1, 2015, was $52,100, determine the balance of Retained Earnings on November 30, 2016.

Requirement 1

General Journal

DATE	ACCOUNT TITLES AND EXPLANATIONS	POST. REF.	DEBIT	CREDIT

Requirement 2

Exercise 13–16 ④

The balance sheet of Nature's Design Technology Inc. reported the following:

Cumulative preferred shares, 300 shares issued and outstanding, liquidation value $15,000	$ 15,000
Common shares, 25,000 shares issued and outstanding	187,500

Assume that Nature's Design had paid preferred dividends for the current year and all prior years (no dividends in arrears). Retained Earnings was $115,000.

Required   Compute the book value per share of the preferred shares and the common shares.

Book value per preferred share:

Book value per common share:

Exercise 13–20 ① ②

Michael Lee has been operating Lee Management Consulting as a proprietorship but is planning to expand operations in the near future. In Chapter 12, Michael had considered taking on a partner but decided not to form a partnership after all. To raise cash for future expansion, he has now decided to incorporate and create Lee Consulting Corporation. He has gone through all the legal steps to incorporate his business; as of August 1, 2016, Lee Consulting Corporation is authorized to issue an unlimited number of common shares and 50,000 $2.00 preferred shares.

The Lee Management Consulting July 31, 2016, balance sheet appears below, adjusted to reflect all amounts at current market value:

Lee Management Consulting Balance Sheet July 31, 2016	
Assets	
Cash	$21,650
Accounts receivable	5,900
Inventory	2,713
Supplies	100
Prepaid rent	6,000
Equipment	1,000
Accumulated amortization—equipment	(75)
Furniture	5,000
Accumulated amortization—furniture	(267)
Total assets	$42,021
Liabilities and Equity	
Accounts payable	$ 9,600
Salary payable	1,000
Unearned service revenue	1,200
Notes payable	0
Michael Lee, capital	30,221
Total liabilities and capital	$42,021

Required

1. Create the journal entry to record the incorporation of the business on August 1, 2016. To do this, you need to record each asset and liability account at its current market value. For equipment and furniture, this would be the net book value of each—there would not be any accumulated amortization accounts at the beginning of the new corporation's life. The Michael Lee, Capital balance would become the value of the 20,000 common shares Michael issues to himself.

2. To raise $50,000 in additional cash, Lee Consulting Corporation issued 1,000 of the preferred shares for $50.00 per share on August 2, 2016. Journalize this transaction.

3. Lee Consulting Corporation incurred $1,500 in legal fees and incorporation fees to organize the corporation under the Canada Business Corporations Act in Ontario. Prepare the journal entry for these organization costs paid on August 5.

Requirements 1 – 3

		General Journal			
DATE		ACCOUNT TITLES AND EXPLANATIONS	POST. REF.	DEBIT	CREDIT

Problem 13–2A ②

The partnership of Nuan Zhang and Jen Phuah needed additional capital to expand into new markets, so the business incorporated as A-1 Services Inc. The articles of incorporation under the Canada Business Corporations Act authorize A-1 Services Inc. to issue 500,000 $2.50 preferred shares and 2,000,000 common shares. In its first year, A-1 Services Inc. completed the following share-related transactions:

2017

Aug.	2	Paid incorporation fees of $6,000 and paid legal fees of $16,000 to organize as a corporation.
	2	Issued 20,000 common shares to Zhang and 25,000 common shares to Phuah in return for cash. Zhang paid $150,000 cash, and Phuah paid $187,500 cash.
Dec.	10	Issued 1,000 preferred shares to acquire a computer system with a market value of $80,000.
	16	Issued 15,000 common shares for cash of $120,000.

Required

1. Record the transactions in the general journal.
2. Prepare the shareholders' equity section of the A-1 Services Inc. balance sheet at December 31, 2017. The ending balance in Retained Earnings is $130,000.

Requirement 1

General Journal

DATE	ACCOUNT TITLES AND EXPLANATIONS	POST. REF.	DEBIT	CREDIT

Requirement 2

Problem 13–4A ② ③

The following summaries for Ruby Distributors Ltd. and Gem Wholesalers Inc. provide the information needed to prepare the shareholders' equity section of each company's balance sheet. The two companies are independent.

Ruby Distributors Ltd. This company is authorized to issue 150,000 common shares. All the shares were issued at $3.00 per share. The company incurred a net loss of $75,000 in 2014 (its first year of operations) and a net loss of $30,000 in 2015. It earned net incomes of $35,000 in 2016 and $60,000 in 2017. The company declared no dividends during the four-year period.

Gem Wholesalers Inc. Gem Wholesalers Inc.'s articles of incorporation authorize the company to issue 200,000 cumulative preferred shares and 1,000,000 common shares. Gem Wholesalers Inc. issued 2,000 preferred shares at $12.50 per share. It issued 100,000 common shares for $300,000. The company's Retained Earnings balance at the beginning of 2017 was $75,000. Net income for 2017 was $50,000, and the company declared the specified preferred share dividend for 2017. Preferred share dividends for 2016 were in arrears. The preferred dividend was $1.10 per share per year.

Required For each company, prepare the shareholders' equity section of its balance sheet at December 31, 2017. Show the computation of all amounts. Journal entries are not required.

Calculations:

Problem 13–6A ③

Rainy Day Corporation has 50,000 $0.50 preferred shares and 600,000 common shares issued and outstanding. During a three-year period, Rainy Day Corporation declared and paid cash dividends as follows: 2014, $0; 2015, $114,000; and 2016, $260,000.

Required

1. Compute the total dividends to preferred shares and common shares for each of the three years if
   a. Preferred shares are noncumulative.
   b. Preferred shares are cumulative.
2. For **Requirement** 1b, record the declaration of the 2016 dividends on December 22, 2016, and the payment of the dividends on January 12, 2017.

Requirement 1a

	Preferred	Common	Total

Requirement 1b

	Preferred	Common	Total

Requirement 2

General Journal

DATE		ACCOUNT TITLES AND EXPLANATIONS	POST. REF.	DEBIT	CREDIT

Problem 13–7A ③ ④

The balance sheet of Tulameen Systems Inc. reported the following:

Shareholders' Equity

Preferred shares, cumulative convertible, authorized 25,000 shares	$200,000
Common shares, authorized 50,000 shares, issued 44,000 shares	528,000
Retained earnings	168,000
Total shareholders' equity	$896,000

Notes to the financial statements indicate that 10,000 $1.20 preferred shares were issued and outstanding. The preferred shares have a liquidation value of $24.00 per share. Preferred dividends are in arrears for two years, including the current year. On the balance sheet date, the market value of the Tulameen Systems Inc. common shares was $28.00 per share.

Required

1. Are the preferred shares cumulative or noncumulative? How can you tell?
2. What is the total contributed capital of the company?
3. What is the total market value of the common shares?
4. Compute the book value per share of the preferred shares and of the common shares.

Requirements 1 – 4

Problem 13–9A ② ⑤

The following accounts and related balances of Etse Manufacturing Inc. are arranged in no particular order:

Accounts Payable	$ 36,000	Accrued Liabilities	$ 23,000
Retained Earnings	?	Long-term Note Payable	100,500
Common Shares,		Accounts Receivable, net	100,000
100,000 shares authorized, 33,000 shares		Preferred Shares, $0.15	
issued and outstanding	165,000	25,000 shares authorized, 6,000 shares issued	30,000
Dividends Payable	4,500	Cash	35,000
Total assets, Dec. 31, 2016	567,500	Inventory	190,500
Net income	140,750	Property, Plant, and Equipment, net	381,000
Common Shareholders' Equity, Dec. 31, 2016	520,000	Prepaid Expenses	15,500
Interest Expense	10,850	Patent, net	37,000

Required

1. Prepare the company's classified balance sheet in the report format at December 31, 2017.

2. Compute the rate of return on total assets and the rate of return on common shareholders' equity for the year ended December 31, 2017.

3. Do these rates of return suggest strength or weakness? Give your reason.

Requirement 1

Requirement 2

Rate of return on total assets:

Rate of return on common shareholders' equity:

Requirement 3

14 CORPORATIONS: RETAINED EARNINGS AND THE INCOME STATEMENT

LEARNING OBJECTIVES

1 Account for stock dividends and stock splits.
2 Account for repurchased shares.
3 Prepare a detailed corporate income statement.
4 Prepare a statement of retained earnings and a statement of shareholders' equity.
5 Identify the impact of IFRS on the income statement and the statement of shareholders' equity.

Starter 14–3 ①

Compare and contrast the accounting for cash dividends and stock dividends. In the space provided, insert either "Cash dividends," "Stock dividends," or "Both cash dividends and stock dividends" to complete each of the following statements:

1. _____ decrease Retained Earnings.

2. _____ have no effect on a liability.

3. _____ increase contributed capital by the same amount that they decrease retained earnings.

4. _____ decrease both total assets and total shareholders' equity, resulting in a decrease in the size of the company.

Starter 14–7 ②

Justice Inc. began 2017 with the following account balances:

Common shares, 150,000 shares authorized,	
75,000 issued	$2,175,000
Retained earnings	820,000

In early 2017, Justice Inc. reported the following transactions:

Jan. 10 Repurchased 7,500 of its own shares for $31 per share.

Feb. 20 Sold 4,000 of the repurchased shares for $32 per share.

Mar. 30 Sold the remaining repurchased shares for $25 per share.

Record journal entries for the above transactions.

General Journal

DATE		ACCOUNT TITLES AND EXPLANATIONS	POST. REF.	DEBIT	CREDIT

Calculations:

Starter 14–12 ③

Figero Inc. has $350,000 of income in 2017. During that same time it declared preferred dividends in the amount of $13,000. The following activities affecting common shares occurred during the year:

Jan.   1   120,000 common shares were outstanding

Aug.   1   Sold 35,000 common shares

Sep.   1   Issued a 10 percent common stock dividend

1. Calculate the weighted average number of common shares outstanding during the year.
2. Calculate earnings per share. Round to the nearest cent.

Requirement 1

Number of Common Shares Outstanding	Fraction of Year	Dates	Weighted Average Number of Common Shares Outstanding
	Weighted average number of common shares outstanding during period =		

Requirement 2

Earnings per share:

Starter 14–17 ④

For each of the following situations, indicate whether there is a change in estimate, a change of policy, or an error by inserting a check mark in the correct box. Then indicate if the correction needs to be applied retrospectively (change past statement information) or prospectively (only future statements will be affected) by checking the correct box in the right two columns.

	Change in Estimate	Change in Policy	Error	Retrospective Statement	Prospective Statement
A switch from the weighted-average method of inventory to the FIFO method.					
Management decided the welding equipment will last 12 years and not the original estimate of 10 years.					
Missing expense invoices were found after the financial statements were finalized.					

Starter 14–21 ⑤

Prepare a simple statement of comprehensive income for Yoshi Corporation using the following information:

- For the year ended June 30, 2017
- Loss for the year is $25,000
- Gain on equity investments is $60,000
- Tax rate is 25 percent

Exercise 14–2 ①

Nguyen Limited reports the following transactions for 2016:

Feb.   1   Sold 6,000 shares of $1.50, noncumulative, preferred shares for $70 per share.

Feb.   20   Sold 30,000 common shares for $9 per share.

Oct.   13   Declared a 10 percent stock dividend on the common shares. The current market price of the common shares is $12 per share. There are 100,000 common shares outstanding on October 13.

Nov.   16   Distributed the stock dividend declared on October 13.

Dec.   11   Declared the annual dividend required on the preferred shares and a $0.35 per share dividend on the common shares. There are 20,000 preferred shares outstanding at this time.

Required   Prepare journal entries for the above transactions. Explanations are not required.

General Journal				
DATE	ACCOUNT TITLES AND EXPLANATIONS	POST. REF.	DEBIT	CREDIT

Exercise 14–3 ①

Poco Travel Ltd. is authorized to issue 500,000 common shares. The company issued 70,000 shares at $7.50 per share. On June 10, 2017, when the Retained Earnings balance was $360,000, Poco Travel Ltd. declared a 10 percent stock dividend using the market value of $4.00 per share. It distributed the stock dividend on July 20, 2017. On August 5, 2017, Poco Travel Ltd. declared a $0.45 per share cash dividend, which it paid on September 15, 2017.

Required

1. Journalize the declaration and distribution of the stock dividend.
2. Journalize the declaration and payment of the cash dividend.
3. Prepare the shareholders' equity section of the balance sheet after both dividends.

Requirements 1 & 2

DATE		ACCOUNT TITLES AND EXPLANATIONS	POST. REF.	DEBIT	CREDIT

General Journal

Requirement 3

Exercise 14–4 ①

Halifax Metal Products Ltd. had the following shareholders' equity at October 31, 2017:

Common shares, unlimited shares authorized, 60,000 shares issued and outstanding	$150,000
Retained earnings	450,000
Total shareholders' equity	$600,000

On November 14, 2017, Halifax Metal Products Ltd. split its common shares 2 for 1. Make the memorandum entry to record the stock split, and prepare the shareholders' equity section of the balance sheet immediately after the split.

Exercise 14–5 ①

Examine Halifax Metal Products Ltd.'s shareholders' equity section for October 31, 2017, in Exercise 14–4. Suppose Halifax Metal Products Ltd. consolidated its common shares 1 for 2 (a reverse stock split) to increase the market price of its shares. The company's shares were trading at $6.00 immediately before the reverse split. Make the memorandum entry to record the share consolidation, and prepare the shareholders' equity section of Halifax Metal Products Ltd.'s balance sheet after the share consolidation. What would you expect the market price to be, approximately, after the reverse split?

Exercise 14–7 ① ②

Identify the effects of these transactions on shareholders' equity. Has shareholders' equity increased, decreased, or remained the same? Each transaction is independent.

a. A 10 percent stock dividend. Before the dividend, 400,000 common shares were outstanding; market value was $7.50 at the time of the dividend.

b. A 2-for-1 stock split. Prior to the split, 50,000 common shares were outstanding.

c. Repurchase of 5,000 common shares at $7.00 per share. The average issue price of these shares was $5.00.

d. Sale of 2,000 repurchased common shares for $6.50 per share.

a. – d.

Exercise 14–9 ②

Debon Ltd. had the following shareholders' equity on March 26, 2017:

Common shares, unlimited shares authorized, 140,000 shares issued and outstanding	$420,000
Retained earnings	475,000
Total shareholders' equity	$895,000

On May 3, 2017, the company repurchased and cancelled 5,000 common shares at $3.50 per share.

1. Journalize this transaction and prepare the shareholders' equity section of the balance sheet at June 30, 2017.
2. How many common shares are outstanding after the share repurchase?

Requirement 1

General Journal

DATE	ACCOUNT TITLES AND EXPLANATIONS	POST. REF.	DEBIT	CREDIT

Requirement 2

Exercise 14–12 ③

The ledger of Pottery Supplies Inc. contains the following information for operations for the year ended September 30, 2017:

Sales revenue	$350,000	Income tax expense—gain on	
Operating expenses		discontinued operations	$ 8,500
(excluding income tax)	67,500	Other loss	22,500
Cost of goods sold	230,000	Income tax expense—	
Gain on discontinued		operating income	10,000
operations	21,000		

Required   Prepare a multi-step income statement for the year ended September 30, 2017. Omit earnings per share. Was 2017 a good year or a bad year for Pottery Supplies Inc.? Explain your answer in terms of the outlook for 2018.

Exercise 14–13 ③

Zelda Solutions Inc. earned net income of $122,000 in 2017. The ledger reveals the following figures:

Preferred shares, $1.50, 4,000 shares issued and outstanding	$ 50,000
Common shares, unlimited shares authorized, 100,000 shares issued	300,000

Required Compute Zelda Solutions Inc.'s EPS for 2017, assuming no changes in the share accounts during the year.

_____

_____

_____

_____

Exercise 14–16 ④

Pacific Hotels Inc., a large hotel chain, had Retained Earnings of $250.0 million at the beginning of 2017. The company showed these figures at December 31, 2017:

	($ millions)
Net income	$75.0
Cash dividends—Preferred	1.5
Common	44.5
Debit to retained earnings due to repurchase of preferred shares	4.0

Required Prepare the statement of retained earnings for Pacific Hotels Inc. for the year ended December 31, 2017.

Exercise 14–18 ③

For the year ended December 31, 2016, Evans Inc. reported the following shareholders' equity:

Common shares, 400,000 shares authorized, 140,000 shares issued and outstanding	$1,400,000
Retained earnings	672,000
Total shareholders' equity	$2,072,000

During 2017, Evans Inc. completed these transactions and events (listed in chronological order):

a. Declared and issued a 10 percent stock dividend. At the time, Evans Inc.'s common shares were quoted at a market price of $11.50 per share.

b. Sold 1,000 common shares for $12.50 per share.

c. Sold 1,000 common shares to employees at $10.00 per share.

d. Net income for the year was $397,500.

e. Declared and paid cash dividends of $140,000.

Required Prepare Evans Inc.'s statement of shareholders' equity for 2017.

	COMMON SHARES	RETAINED EARNINGS	TOTAL SHAREHOLDERS' EQUITY

Exercise 14–20 ② ③

To raise cash for future expansion, Michael Lee incorporated his proprietorship and created Lee Consulting Corporation. The corporation is authorized to issue an unlimited number of common shares and 50,000 $2.00 preferred shares. In July 2016, Michael Lee purchased 20,000 common shares for his proprietorship equity of $30,221 and issued 1,000 of the preferred shares for $50.00 per share to increase his investment in the business.

In August 2016, Lee Consulting Corporation has the following transactions related to its common shares:

Aug. 3   The company sold 1,000 of its common shares for $10.00 per share to a small number of people who believed in the company's potential for profit.

20   The company repurchased 100 of its common shares for $12.00 per share from a shareholder who was having financial difficulties.

30   The company sold 100 common shares for $15.00 per share.

Required

1. Journalize the entries related to the transactions.

2. Calculate the ending balance in the Common Shares account.

3. Prepare the statement of shareholders' equity for August 31, 2016. Assume that net income for the period was $67,500.

Requirement 1

	General Journal				
DATE	ACCOUNT TITLES AND EXPLANATIONS	POST. REF.	DEBIT	CREDIT	

Requirement 2

Common Shares

Requirement 3

	PREFERRED SHARES	COMMON SHARES	RETAINED EARNINGS	TOTAL SHAREHOLDERS' EQUITY

Problem 14–2A ① ②

Assume Frelix Construction Ltd. completed the following selected transactions during the year 2017:

Apr. 19 Declared a cash dividend on the $8.50 preferred shares (3,000 shares outstanding). Declared a $2.00 per share dividend on the 100,000 common shares outstanding. The date of record was May 2, and the payment date was May 25.

May 25 Paid the cash dividends.

Jun. 7 Split the company's 100,000 common shares 2 for 1; one new common share was issued for each old share held.

Jul. 29 Declared a 5 percent stock dividend on the common shares to holders of record on August 22, with distribution set for September 9. The market value was $36.00 per common share.

Sep. 9 Issued the stock dividend shares.

Nov. 26 Repurchased 5,000 of the company's own common shares at $40.00 per share. They had an average issue price of $28.00 per share.

Required   Record the transactions in the general journal.

General Journal

DATE		ACCOUNT TITLES AND EXPLANATIONS	POST. REF.	DEBIT	CREDIT

Problem 14–4A ① ② ③

The information below was taken from the ledger and other records of Stahl Metalworks Corp. at September 30, 2017:

Cost of goods sold	$157,500
Loss on sale of property	17,500
Sales returns	3,500
Income tax expense (saving)	
Continuing operations	13,500
Discontinued segment:	
Operating loss	(1,800)
Gain on sale	600
Gain on sale of discontinued segment	1,750
Interest expense	4,250
General expenses	42,000
Interest revenue	1,750
Preferred shares, $1.00, 15,000 shares authorized, 7,500 shares issued and outstanding	93,750
Retained earnings, October 1, 2016	30,500
Selling expenses	50,750
Common shares, 50,000 shares authorized, issued, and outstanding	165,000
Sales revenue	315,000
Dividends	11,000
Operating loss, discontinued segment	5,250
Loss on insurance settlement	4,000

Required   Prepare a single-step income statement, including earnings per share, for Stahl Metalworks Corp. for the fiscal year ended September 30, 2017. Evaluate income for the year ended September 30, 2017, in terms of the outlook for 2018. Assume 2017 was a typical year and that Stahl Metalworks Corp.'s managers hoped to earn income from continuing operations equal to 10 percent of net sales.

Calculations and Evaluation:

Problem 14–5A ③

The capital structure of Renault Marketing Inc. at December 31, 2016, included 50,000, $0.50 preferred shares and 74,000 common shares. The 50,000 preferred shares were issued in 2009. Common shares outstanding during 2017 were 74,000 January through April and 80,000 May through September. A 20 percent stock dividend was paid on October 1. Income from continuing operations during 2017 was $122,000. The company discontinued a segment of the business at a gain (net of tax) of $9,250. The Renault Marketing Inc. board of directors restricts $125,000 of retained earnings for contingencies.

Required

1. Compute Renault Marketing Inc.'s earnings per share. Start with income from continuing operations. Income of $122,000 is net of income tax.

2. Show two ways of reporting Renault Marketing Inc.'s retained earnings restriction. Retained Earnings at December 31, 2016, was $145,500, and total contributed capital at December 31, 2017, is $375,000. The company declared dividends of $49,500 in 2017.

Calculations:

Requirement 1

Requirement 2

Requirement 2 (Continued)

Problem 14–8A ① ② ④

Timpano Communication Inc. had the following shareholders' equity on January 1, 2017:

Preferred shares, $2.00, cumulative (1 year in arrears), liquidation price of $20, 100,000 shares authorized, 15,000 shares issued and outstanding	$240,000
Common shares, unlimited number of shares authorized, 25,000 shares issued and outstanding	200,000
Total contributed capital	440,000
Retained earnings	512,000
Total shareholders' equity	$952,000

The following transactions took place during 2017:

Jan.	14	Declared a $90,000 cash dividend, payable on March 1 to the shareholders of record on February 1. Indicate the amount payable to each class of shareholder.
Feb.	28	Issued 10,000 common shares for $6.00 per share.
Mar.	1	Paid the cash dividend declared on January 14.
Apr.	1	Declared a 10 percent stock dividend on the common shares, distributable on May 2 to the shareholders of record on April 15. The market value of the shares was $6.40 per share.
May	2	Distributed the stock dividend declared on April 1.
Jul.	4	Repurchased 3,000 of the company's own common shares at $7.00 per share.
Sep.	2	Issued 2,500 common shares for $7.50 per share.
Nov.	2	Split the common shares 2 for 1.
Dec.	31	Reported net income of $250,000. Closed the Income Summary account.

Required

1. Record the transactions in the general journal. Explanations are not required.
2. Prepare the statement of shareholders' equity for the year ended December 31, 2017.

Calculations:

Requirement 1

	General Journal			
DATE	ACCOUNT TITLES AND EXPLANATIONS	POST. REF.	DEBIT	CREDIT

Requirement 2

	PREFERRED SHARES	COMMON SHARES	CONTRIBUTED SURPLUS—SHARE REPURCHASE	RETAINED EARNINGS	TOTAL SHAREHOLDERS' EQUITY

Problem 14–9A ① ③ ④

ArtnMotion Inc. specializes in truck tires and had the following shareholders' equity on January 1, 2017:

Preferred shares, $2.50, convertible to common on a 2-for-1 basis, 100,000 shares authorized, 50,000 shares issued and outstanding	$1,500,000
Common shares, unlimited number of shares authorized, 150,000 shares issued and outstanding	1,500,000
Total contributed capital	3,000,000
Retained earnings	1,200,000
Total shareholders' equity	$4,200,000

The following information is available for the year ending December 31, 2017:

Feb. 1   Declared a cash dividend of $275,000, payable on March 1 to the shareholders of record on February 15. Indicate the amount payable to each class of shareholder.

Mar. 1   Paid the cash dividend declared on February 1.

May 2   Declared a 20 percent stock dividend on the common shares, distributable on July 4 to the shareholders of record on June 15. The market value of the shares was $11.00 per share.

Jul. 4   Distributed the common shares dividend declared on May 2.

Aug. 8   The company discovered that amortization expense recorded in 2015 was understated in error by $30,000. (Ignore any tax consequences.)

Dec. 31   ArtnMotion Inc.'s records show the following:

Sales for the year	$3,150,000
Cost of goods sold	1,290,000
Operating expenses	792,000
Income from discontinued operations	132,000
Loss on sale of discontinued operations	76,000

Close only the Income Summary account, assuming the company pays taxes at the rate of 35 percent.

Required

1. Record the transactions in the general journal. Explanations are not required.
2. Prepare a combined statement of income and retained earnings for the year ended December 31, 2017. Include earnings per share information. For purposes of the earnings per share calculation, the weighted average number of common shares is 180,000.

Requirement 1

General Journal

DATE	ACCOUNT TITLES AND EXPLANATIONS	POST. REF.	DEBIT	CREDIT

Requirement 2

15 LONG-TERM LIABILITIES

LEARNING OBJECTIVES

1 Define bonds payable and the types of bonds.
2 Determine the price of a bond, and account for basic bond transactions.
3 Amortize a bond discount and premium by the straight-line amortization method and the effective-interest amortization method.
4 Account for retirement and conversion of bonds.
5 Show the advantages and disadvantages of borrowing.
6 Account for other long-term liabilities.
7 Account for operating leases and for assets acquired through a capital lease.
8 Identify the effects of IFRS on long-term liabilities.

*A1 Compute the future value of an investment.
*A2 Compute the present value of a single future amount and the present value of an annuity.

Starter 15–1 ①

Match the following terms by entering in the blank space the letter of the phrase that best describes each term.

Bond terms and definitions

_____ Bond indenture   _____ Unregistered bonds

_____ Secured bonds   _____ Bearer bonds

_____ Debentures   _____ Serial bonds

_____ Convertible bonds   _____ Redeemable bonds

_____ Over-the-counter market   _____ Market interest rate

_____ Bond discount   _____ Bond premium

_____ Contract interest rate

a. Interest rate that investors demand in order to loan their money
b. May be converted into the company's common shares
c. Matures in instalments over a period of time
d. Unsecured bond backed only by the good faith of the issuer
e. Contract agreed to between the issuer of the bonds and the purchaser
f. Excess of a bond's maturity value over its issue price
g. Assets of the issuer are provided as collateral
h. Another name for bearer bonds
i. Interest rate that determines the amount of cash interest the borrower pays and the investor receives each year
j. Principal is payable to the person that has possession of the bonds
k. Bonds that give the buyer an option of retiring the bonds before maturity
l. A place where bonds are bought and sold by investors
m. Excess of a bond's issue price over its par value

Starter 15–2 ②

Determine the present value of a $1,000 bond payable issued at maturity value, at a premium, or at a discount (interest is payable annually on this 10-year bond) in each of the situations below.

a. The market interest rate is 7 percent. Jersey Corp. issues bonds payable with a stated rate of 6.5 percent.

b. Frobisher Bay Inc. issued 7 percent bonds payable when the market rate was 6.75 percent.

c. Carola Corporation issued 8 percent bonds when the market interest rate was 8 percent.

d. Black Hawk Corp. issued bonds payable that pay stated interest of 7 percent. At issuance, the market interest rate was 8.25 percent.

a. – d.

Starter 15–11 ② ③

Surf Sisters Corp. issued a $400,000, 7 percent, 10-year bond payable at a price of 105 on January 1, 2017. Journalize the following transactions for Surf Sisters Corp. Include an explanation for each entry.

1. Issuance of the bond payable on January 1, 2017.

2. Payment of semi-annual interest and amortization of bond premium on July 1, 2017. Surf Sisters uses the straight-line method to amortize the premium.

Requirements 1 & 2

General Journal				
DATE	ACCOUNT TITLES AND EXPLANATIONS	POST. REF.	DEBIT	CREDIT

Starter 15–12 ③

Live Nation Inc. issued $1,500,000 of 6 percent, 10-year bonds payable and received cash proceeds of $1,388,419 on March 31, 2017. The market interest rate at the date of issuance was 7 percent, and the bonds pay interest semi-annually.

1. Did the bonds sell at a premium or a discount?
2. Prepare an effective-interest amortization table for the bond discount through the first two interest payments. Use Exhibit 15–5 as a guide, and round amounts to the nearest dollar. Students can use a financial calculator if so instructed.
3. Record Live Nation Inc.'s issuance of the bonds on March 31, 2017, and payment of the first semi-annual interest amount and amortization of the bond discount on September 30, 2017. Explanations are not required.
4. If we were to amortize the bond discount using the straight-line method instead of the effective-interest method, record the first interest amortization entry.

Requirement 1

Requirement 2

SEMI-ANNUAL INTEREST PERIOD	A INTEREST PAYMENT (% OF MATURITY VALUE)	B INTEREST EXPENSE (% OF PRECEDING BOND CARRYING AMOUNT)	C DISCOUNT AMORTIZATION (B – A)	D UNAMORTIZED DISCOUNT ACCOUNT BALANCE (Previous D – Current C)	E BOND CARRYING AMOUNT (Bond – D)

Requirement 3

General Journal

DATE		ACCOUNT TITLES AND EXPLANATIONS	POST. REF.	DEBIT	CREDIT

Requirement 4

General Journal

DATE		ACCOUNT TITLES AND EXPLANATIONS	POST. REF.	DEBIT	CREDIT

Starter 15–17 ③ ⑥

Talon Inc. includes the following selected accounts in its general ledger at December 31, 2017:

Notes Payable, Long-Term......................................	$ 60,000	Accounts Payable..	$ 26,000
Bonds Payable...	100,000	Discount on Bonds Payable................................	3,000
Interest Payable (due next year)..	500	Mortgage Payable (payments are $1,000 per month)..	100,000

Prepare the liabilities section of Talon Inc.'s balance sheet at December 31, 2017, to show how the company would report these items. Report a total for current liabilities.

Starter 15–19 ④

On January 1, 2017, Thames Company purchases a vehicle and signs a six-year loan for $60,000 at 4 percent. Complete the partial amortization schedule below assuming they will make a monthly payment of $980:

Payment Number	Date	Equal Payment	Interest Expense	Principal Portion	Balance
	Jan. 1, 2017				60,000.00
1	Jan. 31, 2017				
2	Feb. 28, 2017				
3	Mar. 31, 2017				
4	Apr. 30, 2017				
5	May 31, 2017				
6	Jun. 30, 2017				

At the end of 2017, what amount would be shown on the balance sheet for the current portion of the loan?

Starter 15–20 ⑦

Best Corp. agrees to lease a store in a mall and open a coffee shop. On January 2, 2017, the company pays a non-refundable $20,000 deposit to secure the store and agrees to a lease amount of $10,000 per month for two years. Journalize the initial lease deposit, the first monthly lease payment, and the December 31 year-end adjustment of the $20,000 deposit. Explanations are not required. Would Best Corp. report the lease information in the notes to the financial statements? Why or why not?

General Journal

DATE		ACCOUNT TITLES AND EXPLANATIONS	POST. REF.	DEBIT	CREDIT

Starter 15–21 ⑧

Briefly answer the following questions:

a. When accounting for bonds, what is the primary difference between ASPE and IFRS?

b. When accounting for leases, what is the primary difference between ASPE and IFRS?

a. & b.

_____

_____

_____

_____

_____

_____

_____

_____

Exercise 15–5 ② ③

Saturna Corp. issues 20-year, 6 percent bonds with a maturity value of $5,000,000 on April 30. The bonds sell at par and pay interest on March 31 and September 30. Record (a) the issuance of the bonds on April 30, (b) the payment of interest on September 30, and (c) the accrual of interest on December 31.

a. – c.

		General Journal			
DATE		ACCOUNT TITLES AND EXPLANATIONS	POST. REF.	DEBIT	CREDIT

Exercise 15–9 ③

Life Fitness Ltd. is authorized to issue $6,000,000 of 5 percent, 10-year bonds. On January 2, 2017, the contract date, when the market interest rate is 6 percent, the company issues $4,800,000 of the bonds and receives cash of $4,442,941. Interest is paid on June 30 and December 31 each year. Life Fitness Ltd. amortizes bond discounts by the effective-interest method.

Required

1. Prepare an amortization table for the first four semi-annual interest periods. Follow the format of Panel B in Exhibit 15–5 on page 852.
2. Record the issue of the bonds on January 2, the first semi-annual interest payment on June 30, and the second payment on December 31.
3. Show the balance sheet presentation of the bond on the date of issue and on December 31, 2018.

Requirement 1

SEMI-ANNUAL INTEREST PERIOD	A INTEREST PAYMENT (% OF MATURITY VALUE)	B INTEREST EXPENSE (% OF PRECEDING BOND CARRYING AMOUNT)	C DISCOUNT AMORTIZATION (B – A)	D UNAMORTIZED DISCOUNT ACCOUNT BALANCE (Previous D – Current C)	E BOND CARRYING AMOUNT (Bond – D)

Requirement 2

General Journal

DATE	ACCOUNT TITLES AND EXPLANATIONS	POST. REF.	DEBIT	CREDIT

Requirement 3

Exercise 15–10 ③

On September 30, 2017, when the market interest rate is 6 percent, LeHigh Ltd. issues $8,000,000 of 8 percent, 20-year bonds for $9,849,182. The bonds pay interest on March 31 and September 30. Lehigh Ltd. amortizes a bond premium by the effective-interest method.

Required

1. Prepare an amortization table for the first four semi-annual interest periods. Follow the format of Panel B in Exhibit 15–7 on page 854.

2. Record the issuance of the bonds on September 30, 2017, the accrual of interest at December 31, 2017, and the semi-annual interest payment on March 31, 2018.

Requirement 1

SEMI-ANNUAL INTEREST PERIOD	A INTEREST PAYMENT (% OF MATURITY VALUE)	B INTEREST EXPENSE (% OF PRECEDING BOND CARRYING AMOUNT)	C PREMIUM AMORTIZATION (B – A)	D UNAMORTIZED PREMIUM ACCOUNT BALANCE (Previous D – Current C)	E BOND CARRYING AMOUNT (Bond + D)

Requirement 2

General Journal

DATE		ACCOUNT TITLES AND EXPLANATIONS	POST. REF.	DEBIT	CREDIT

Exercise 15–12 ④

Saint Martin Inc. issued $300,000, 12 percent, 10-year bonds on July 1, 2016. Interest payments dates are January 2 and July 1. The issue price was $293,400. The bonds are convertible into common shares at the rate of 15 common shares for each $1,000 bond. The market price of Saint Martin Inc. common shares has risen steadily over the past two years, and on July 1, 2018, half of the bonds are converted into common shares.

Required

1. Compute the balance in the premium or discount account on the date of conversion. Saint Martin Inc. uses the straight-line method of amortization.

2. Prepare the entry to convert half of the bonds into common shares.

Requirement 1

_____

_____

_____

_____

_____

Requirement 2

General Journal

DATE		ACCOUNT TITLES AND EXPLANATIONS	POST. REF.	DEBIT	CREDIT

Exercise 15–17 (5)

Pudong Transport Ltd. is considering two plans for raising $4,000,000 to expand operations. Plan A is to borrow at 9 percent, and Plan B is to issue 400,000 common shares. Before any new financing, Pudong Transport Ltd. has net income after interest and income tax of $2,000,000 and 400,000 common shares outstanding. Management believes the company can use the new funds to earn income of $840,000 per year before interest and taxes. The income tax rate is 35 percent.

Required Analyze Pudong Transport Ltd.'s situation to determine which plan will result in higher earnings per share. Use Exhibit 15–9 on page 861 as a guide.

	PLAN A BORROW $4,000,000 AT 9%	PLAN B ISSUE $400,000 OF COMMON SHARES
Net income after interest and income tax, before expansion		
Project income before interest and income tax		
Interest expense		
Project income before income tax		
Income tax on new project (35%)		
Project net income		
Total company net income		
Earnings per share including expansion		
Plan A		
Plan B		

Exercise 15–22 ⑦

A capital lease agreement for equipment requires Granger Transport Ltd. to make 10 annual payments of $40,000, with the first payment due on January 2, 2017, the date of the inception of the lease. The present value of the nine future lease payments at 10 percent is $230,360.

Required

1. Calculate the present value of the lease at 5 percent if your instructor has taught present value.

2. Journalize the following lessee transactions:

2017

Jan.   2   Beginning of lease term and first annual payment.

Dec.   31   Amortization of equipment (10 percent).

        31   Interest expense on lease liability.

2018

Jan.   2   Second annual lease payment.

3. Assume now that this is an operating lease. Journalize the January 2, 2017, lease payment.

Requirement 1

Requirements 2 & 3

General Journal

DATE		ACCOUNT TITLES AND EXPLANATIONS	POST. REF.	DEBIT	CREDIT

Exercise 15–23 ②

Lee Consulting Corporation is considering raising capital for a planned business expansion to a new market. Lee believes the company will need $500,000 and plans to raise the capital by issuing 6 percent, 10-year bonds on April 1, 2017. The bonds pay interest semi-annually on April 1 and October 1. On April 1, 2017, the market rate of interest required by similar bonds by investors is 8 percent, causing the bonds to sell for $431,850.

Required

1. Were the Lee Consulting Corporation bonds issued at par, at a premium, or at a discount?

2. Record the cash received on the bond issue date.

3. Journalize the first interest payment on October 1, 2017, and amortize the premium or discount using the effective-interest method.

4. Journalize the entry required, if any, on December 31, 2017, related to the bonds.

Requirement 1

Requirement 2

General Journal

DATE	ACCOUNT TITLES AND EXPLANATIONS	POST. REF.	DEBIT	CREDIT

Requirement 3

General Journal

DATE		ACCOUNT TITLES AND EXPLANATIONS	POST. REF.	DEBIT	CREDIT

Requirement 4

General Journal

DATE		ACCOUNT TITLES AND EXPLANATIONS	POST. REF.	DEBIT	CREDIT

Problem 15–2A ② ③

On March 1, 2017, Shaw Systems Ltd. issues 8.5 percent, 20-year bonds payable with a maturity value of $5,000,000. The bonds pay interest on February 28 and August 31. Shaw Systems Ltd. amortizes premiums and discounts by the straight-line method.

Required

1. If the market interest rate is 7.5 percent when Shaw Systems issues its bonds, will the bonds be priced at par, at a premium, or at a discount? Explain.

2. If the market interest rate is 9 percent when Shaw Systems issues its bonds, will the bonds be priced at par, at a premium, or at a discount? Explain.

3. Assume the issue price of the bonds is 97.00. Journalize the following bond transactions:

   a. Issuance of the bonds on March 1, 2017.

   b. Payment of interest and amortization of the discount on August 31, 2017.

   c. Accrual of interest and amortization of the discount on December 31, 2017, Shaw Systems' year end.

   d. Payment of interest and amortization of the discount on February 28, 2018.

4. Report interest payable and bonds payable as they would appear on the Shaw Systems Ltd. balance sheet at December 31, 2017.

Requirements 1 & 2

Requirement 3 a. – d.

General Journal

DATE		ACCOUNT TITLES AND EXPLANATIONS	POST. REF.	DEBIT	CREDIT

Calculations:

Requirement 4

Problem 15–4A ② ③ ④

On December 31, 2017, Belagio Holdings Ltd. issues 6 percent, 10-year convertible bonds with a maturity value of $6,000,000. The semi-annual interest dates are June 30 and December 31. The market interest rate is 5 percent and the issue price of the bonds is 107.79458. Belagio Holdings Ltd. amortizes any bond premium and discount by the effective-interest method.

Required

1. Prepare an effective-interest-method amortization table for the first four semi-annual interest periods.
2. Journalize the following transactions:
   a. Issuance of the bonds on December 31, 2017. Credit Convertible Bonds Payable.
   b. Payment of interest on June 30, 2018.
   c. Payment of interest on December 31, 2018.
   d. Retirement of bonds with maturity value of $3,000,000 on July 2, 2019. Belagio Holdings pays the call price of 104.00.
   e. Conversion by the bondholders on July 2, 2019, of bonds with maturity value of $2,000,000 into 40,000 of Belagio Holdings Ltd. common shares.
3. Prepare the balance sheet presentation of the bonds payable that are outstanding at December 31, 2019.

Requirement 1

SEMI-ANNUAL INTEREST PERIOD	A INTEREST PAYMENT (% OF MATURITY VALUE)	B INTEREST EXPENSE (% OF PRECEDING BOND CARRYING AMOUNT)	C PREMIUM AMORTIZATION (B – A)	D UNAMORTIZED PREMIUM ACCOUNT BALANCE (Previous D – Current C)	E BOND CARRYING AMOUNT (Bond + D)

Requirement 2

General Journal

DATE		ACCOUNT TITLES AND EXPLANATIONS	POST. REF.	DEBIT	CREDIT

Requirement 3

Problem 15–5A ② ③ ④

Shield Transport Ltd. is authorized to issue 10-year, 6 percent convertible bonds with a maturity value of $16,000,000. Interest is payable on June 30 and December 31. The bonds are convertible on the basis of 50 common shares for each $1,000 bond. The following bond transactions took place:

2017

Jan.   2   Issued bonds with $6,400,000 maturity value. Since the market rate of interest on this date was 8 percent, the bonds sold for $5,530,219.

Jun.   30   Paid semi-annual interest and amortized the discount using the effective-interest amortization method.

Dec.   31   Paid semi-annual interest and amortized the discount using the effective-interest amortization method.

2018

Jun.   30   Paid semi-annual interest and amortized the discount using the effective-interest amortization method.

Jul.   2   Retired bonds with a $3,200,000 maturity value at a rate of 94.00.

       2   Bondholders converted bonds with a $1,600,000 maturity value into common shares.

Required

1. Create an amortization schedule for the first three interest periods for the bonds sold on January 2, 2017. Round all amounts to the nearest whole dollar. Use the values from the schedule and any other information to journalize all the transactions above.

2. Show the balance sheet presentation of the bonds payable on July 2, 2018.

Requirement 1

SEMI-ANNUAL INTEREST PERIOD	A INTEREST PAYMENT (% OF MATURITY VALUE)	B INTEREST EXPENSE (% OF PRECEDING BOND CARRYING AMOUNT)	C DISCOUNT AMORTIZATION (B – A)	D UNAMORTIZED DISCOUNT ACCOUNT BALANCE (Previous D – Current C)	E BOND CARRYING AMOUNT (Bond – D)

Requirement 1 (Continued)

General Journal

DATE		ACCOUNT TITLES AND EXPLANATIONS	POST. REF.	DEBIT	CREDIT

Requirement 2

Problem 15–7A ⑥

Domaine Wines Ltd. issued an $800,000, 5-year, 6 percent mortgage note payable on December 31, 2017, to help finance a new warehouse. The terms of the mortgage provide for semi-annual blended payments of $93,784 on June 30 and December 31 of each year.

1. Prepare a mortgage instalment payment schedule for the first two years of this mortgage. Round all amounts to the nearest whole dollar.

2. Record the issuance of the mortgage note payable on December 31, 2017.

3. Report interest payable and the mortgage note payable on the December 31, 2017, balance sheet.

4. Journalize the first two instalment payments on June 30, 2018, and December 31, 2018.

Requirement 1

SEMI-ANNUAL INTEREST PERIOD	A PAYMENT	B INTEREST EXPENSE	C REDUCTION OF PRINCIPAL	D PRINCIPAL BALANCE

Requirement 2

General Journal

DATE	ACCOUNT TITLES AND EXPLANATIONS	POST. REF.	DEBIT	CREDIT

Requirement 3

Requirement 4

General Journal

DATE		ACCOUNT TITLES AND EXPLANATIONS	POST. REF.	DEBIT	CREDIT

*Problem 15A–2 (A1) (A2)

For each situation, compute the required amount using the tables in this appendix.

1. XS Technologies Inc.'s operations are generating excess cash that will be invested in a special fund. During 2017, XS Technologies invests $12,000,000 in the fund for a planned advertising campaign for a new product to be released six years later, in 2023. If XS Technologies's investments can earn 5 percent each year, how much cash will the company have for the advertising campaign in 2023?

2. XS Technologies Inc. will need $20 million to advertise a new product in 2019. How much must XS Technologies invest in 2017 to have the cash available for the advertising campaign? XS Technologies's investments can earn 5 percent annually.

3. Explain the relationship between your answers to (1) and (2).

EXHIBIT 15A–6   Present Value of $1

Periods	2%	3%	4%	5%
1	0.980	0.971	0.962	0.952
2	0.961	0.943	0.925	0.907
3	0.942	0.915	0.889	0.864
4	0.924	0.889	0.855	0.823
5	0.906	0.863	0.822	0.784
6	0.888	0.838	0.790	0.746
7	0.871	0.813	0.760	0.711
8	0.854	0.789	0.731	0.677
9	0.837	0.766	0.703	0.645
10	0.820	0.744	0.676	0.614

EXHIBIT 15A–7   Present Value of Annuity of $1

Periods	2%	3%	4%	5%
1	0.980	0.971	0.962	0.952
2	1.942	1.914	1.886	1.859
3	2.884	2.829	2.775	2.723
4	3.808	3.717	3.630	3.546
5	4.714	4.580	4.452	4.329
6	5.601	5.417	5.242	5.076
7	6.472	6.230	6.002	5.786
8	7.326	7.020	6.733	6.463
9	8.162	7.786	7.435	7.108
10	8.983	8.530	8.111	7.722

Requirements 1 – 3

16 INVESTMENTS AND INTERNATIONAL OPERATIONS

LEARNING OBJECTIVES

1 Account for short-term investments.
2 Account for long-term share investments.
3 Use the equity method to account for investments.
4 Describe and create consolidated financial statements.
5 Account for investments in bonds.
6 Account for foreign-currency transactions.
7 Identify the impact of IFRS on accounting for investments and international transactions.

Starter 16–3 ①

McBain Electronics completed the following investment transactions during 2016 and 2017:

2016

Dec.	12	Purchased 1,500 shares of Blackmore Ltd. at a price of $62.00 per share, intending to sell the investment within the next year. Commissions were $510.
	21	Received a cash dividend of $0.48 per share on the Blackmore Ltd. shares.
	31	Adjusted the investment to its fair value of $61.50 per share.

2017

Jan.	16	Sold the Blackmore Ltd. shares for $59.00 per share, less commissions of $490.

1. Classify McBain's investment as short term or long term.
2. Journalize McBain's investment transactions. Explanations are not required.

Requirement 1

_____

_____

_____

_____

_____

_____

_____

Requirement 2

		General Journal			
DATE		ACCOUNT TITLES AND EXPLANATIONS	POST. REF.	DEBIT	CREDIT

Starter 16–5 ②

Gerber Ltd. buys 2,000 of the 100,000 shares of Efron Inc., paying $35.00 per share. Suppose Efron distributes a 10 percent stock dividend. Later the same year, Gerber Ltd. sells the Efron shares for $29.00 per share. Disregard commissions on the purchase and sale.

1. Compute Gerber Ltd.'s new cost per share after receiving the stock dividend.
2. Compute Gerber Ltd.'s gain or loss on the sale of this long-term investment.

Requirements 1 & 2

Starter 16–8 ③

Suppose on January 6, 2017, Ling Corp. paid $5,000,000 for its 40 percent investment in True World Inc. Assume True World earned net income of $1,800,000 and paid cash dividends of $800,000 during 2017. Disregard commissions.

1. What method should Ling Corp. use to account for the investment in True World Inc.? Give your reason.
2. Journalize these three transactions on the books of Ling Corp. Include an explanation for each entry.
3. Post to the Investment in True World Inc. Common Shares T-account. What is its balance after all the transactions are posted?

Requirement 1

Requirement 2

General Journal

DATE		ACCOUNT TITLES AND EXPLANATIONS	POST. REF.	DEBIT	CREDIT

Requirement 3

Investment in True World Inc. Common Shares

Starter 16–11 ⑤

Heinz Ltd. owns vast amounts of corporate bonds. Suppose the company buys $1,000,000 of Kuzawa Corporation bonds on January 2, 2017, at a price of 97. The Kuzawa bonds pay cash interest at the annual rate of 6 percent and mature on December 31, 2021.

1. How much did Heinz Ltd. pay to purchase the bond investment? How much will Heinz Ltd. collect when the bond investment matures?

2. How much cash interest will Heinz Ltd. receive each year from Kuzawa Corporation?

3. Compute Heinz Ltd.'s annual interest revenue on this bond investment. Use the straight-line method to amortize the discount on the investment.

Requirements 1 – 3

Starter 16–13 ⑥

Suppose Fleetstar Ltd. sells athletic shoes to a German company on March 14. Fleetstar agrees to accept 2,000,000 euros. On the date of sale, the euro is quoted at $1.56. Fleetstar collects half the receivable on April 19, when the euro is worth $1.55. Then, on May 10, when the price of the euro is $1.58, Fleetstar collects the final amount.

Journalize these three transactions for Fleetstar; include an explanation. Overall, did Fleetstar have a net foreign-currency gain or loss?

	General Journal			
DATE	ACCOUNT TITLES AND EXPLANATIONS	POST. REF.	DEBIT	CREDIT

Starter 16–14 ⑦

Fill in the blanks to indicate how investments are reported under IFRS:

a. Financial instruments are measured at _____.

b. Gains or losses on equity investments with no significant influence are recorded under _____.

c. Significant influence is a rebuttable assumption. It is presumed that if an investor holds (directly or indirectly) _____ or more of the votes.

d. Joint ventures are accounted for using the _____ method.

e. Minority interest is shown on the balance sheet _____ but separate from the parent's _____.

f. Short-term investments in bonds are measured and reported at _____.

g. Long-term investments in bonds are amortized using the _____.

Exercise 16–3 ①

Suppose Carlton Ltd. completed the following investment transactions in 2017 and 2018:

2017

Nov. 6   Purchased 2,000 McGill Corporation common shares for $60,000. Carlton plans to sell the shares in the near future to meet its operating cash flow requirements. Commissions on the purchase were $800.

  30   Received a quarterly cash dividend of $1.50 per share on the McGill Corporation shares.

Dec. 31   Current fair value of the McGill common shares is $62,000.

2018

Jan. 20   Sold the McGill Corporation shares for $63,000, less commissions on the sale of $900.

Required

1. Make the entries to record Carlton Ltd.'s investment transactions. Explanations are not required. Carlton Ltd.'s year end is December 31.

2. Show how Carlton Ltd. would report its investment in the McGill Corporation shares on the balance sheet at December 31, 2017.

Requirement 1

General Journal

DATE		ACCOUNT TITLES AND EXPLANATIONS	POST. REF.	DEBIT	CREDIT

Requirement 2

Exercise 16–5 ②

Journalize the following investment transactions of Vantage Inc.:

Aug. 6   Purchased 900 Rhodes Corporation common shares as a long-term investment, paying $90.00 per share. Vantage Inc. exerts no significant influence on Rhodes Corporation. Commissions on the purchase were $900.

Sep. 12   Received cash dividends of $1.60 per share on the Rhodes Corporation investment.

Nov. 23   Received 90 Rhodes Corporation common shares in a 10 percent stock dividend.

Dec. 4   Unexpectedly sold all the Rhodes Corporation shares for $88.00 per share, less commissions on the sale of $750.

General Journal

DATE	ACCOUNT TITLES AND EXPLANATIONS	POST. REF.	DEBIT	CREDIT

Exercise 16–6 ③

Kinross Gold Corp., introduced in the chapter-opening story, owns equity method investments in several companies. Suppose Kinross paid $12,000,000 to acquire a 40 percent investment in Minecraft Ltd. Further, assume Minecraft Ltd. reported net income of $1,780,000 for the first year and declared and paid cash dividends of $650,000. Record the following entries in Kinross's general journal: (a) purchase of the investment, (b) Kinross's proportion of Minecraft Ltd.'s net income, and (c) receipt of the cash dividends. Disregard commissions on the purchase.

General Journal

DATE	ACCOUNT TITLES AND EXPLANATIONS	POST. REF.	DEBIT	CREDIT

Exercise 16–7 ③

Using the information from Exercise 16–6, calculate the balance in the Investment in Minecraft Ltd. Common Shares T-account. Assume that after all the above transactions took place, Kinross sold its entire investment in Minecraft Ltd. common shares for $13,100,000 cash. Journalize the sale of the investment. Disregard commissions on sale.

Investment in Minecraft Ltd. Common Shares

General Journal					
DATE		ACCOUNT TITLES AND EXPLANATIONS	POST. REF.	DEBIT	CREDIT

Exercise 16–9 ④

Penfold Ltd. owns all the common shares of Simmons Ltd. Prepare a consolidation worksheet using the following information. Assume that the fair value of the assets and liabilities of Simmons Ltd. are equal to their book values.

	PENFOLD LTD.	SIMMONS LTD.	ELIMINATION DEBIT	ELIMINATION CREDIT	CONSOLIDATED AMOUNTS
Assets					
Cash	225,000	55,000			
Accounts receivable, net	360,000	264,000			
Note receivable from Simmons Ltd.	76,000				
Inventory	258,000	159,000			
Investment in Simmons Ltd.	2,350,000				
Property, plant, and equipment, net	3,590,000	2,900,000			
Goodwill					
Total assets	6,859,000	3,378,000			
Liabilities and Shareholders' Equity					
Accounts payable	357,000	180,000			
Notes payable	462,000	759,000			
Other liabilities	78,000	210,000			
Common shares	1,980,000	670,000			
Retained earnings	3,982,000	1,559,000			
	6,859,000	3,378,000			

Exercise 16–10 ④

Pettigrew Holdings Ltd. owns an 80 percent interest in Shortland Inc. Prepare a consolidation worksheet using the information below. Assume that the fair values of Shortland Inc.'s assets and liabilities are equal to their book values.

	PETTIGREW HOLDINGS LTD.	SHORTLAND INC.	ELIMINATION DEBIT	ELIMINATION CREDIT	CONSOLIDATED AMOUNTS
Assets					
Cash	96,000	36,000			
Accounts receivable, net	210,000	144,000			
Note receivable from Shortland Inc.	60,000				
Inventory	246,000	216,000			
Investment in Shortland Inc.	228,000	—			
Property, plant, and equipment, net	720,000	312,000			
Other assets	48,000	42,000			
Goodwill					
Total	1,608,000	750,000			
Liabilities and Shareholders' Equity					
Accounts payable	108,000	66,000			
Notes payable	120,000	96,000			
Other liabilities	204,000	324,000			
Non-controlling interest	—	—			
Common shares	780,000	204,000			
Retained earnings	396,000	60,000			
Total	1,608,000	750,000			

Exercise 16–12 ⑤

On March 31, 2017, Kingpin Corp. paid 98.25 for 4 percent bonds of Claim Limited as an investment. The maturity value of the bonds is $100,000 at September 30, 2021; they pay interest on March 31 and September 30. At December 31, 2017, the bonds' market value is 99.25. The company plans to hold the bonds until they mature.

Required

1. How should Kingpin Corp. account for the bonds?
2. Using the straight-line method of amortizing the discount, journalize all transactions on the bonds for 2017.
3. Show how the investment would be reported by Kingpin Corp. on the balance sheet at December 31, 2017.

Requirement 1

_____

_____

_____

_____

_____

_____

Requirement 2

General Journal

DATE	ACCOUNT TITLES AND EXPLANATIONS	POST. REF.	DEBIT	CREDIT

Requirement 3

_____

_____

_____

_____

_____

_____

_____

Exercise 16–13 ⑤

Ace Properties Ltd. purchased a five-year, 4.5 percent Scotia bond on May 1, 2017, and intends to hold it until it matures. The market rate at the time was 5.2 percent. Interest is paid annually each April 30. Information about the bond appears in the table below. Journalize the purchase and the April 30, 2018, entries. Assume there were no brokerage fees.

Annual Interest Period	Interest Revenue 4.50%	Period Interest Revenue	Discount Amort.	Discount Balance	Bond Carrying Value
May 1, 2017				$30,100	$ 969,900
April 30, 2018	$ 45,000	$ 50,435	$ 5,435	24,665	975,335
April 30, 2019	45,000	50,717	5,717	18,948	981,052
April 30, 2020	45,000	51,015	6,015	12,933	987,067
April 30, 2021	45,000	51,327	6,327	6,606	993,394
April 30, 2022	45,000	51,606	6,606	0	1,000,000
Total	$225,000	$255,100	$30,100		

		General Journal			
DATE		ACCOUNT TITLES AND EXPLANATIONS	POST. REF.	DEBIT	CREDIT

Exercise 16–14 ⑥

Journalize the following foreign-currency transactions for Kingsway Import Inc.:

2017

Nov. 17   Purchased goods on account from a Japanese company. The price was 500,000 yen, and the exchange rate of the yen was $0.0117.

Dec. 16   Paid the Japanese supplier when the exchange rate was $0.0120.

    19   Sold merchandise on account to a French company at a price of 80,000 euros. The exchange rate was $1.57.

    31   Adjusted for the decrease in the value of the euro, which had an exchange rate of $1.54. Kingsway Import Inc.'s year end is December 31.

2018

Jan. 14   Collected from the French company. The exchange rate was $1.58.

General Journal

DATE		ACCOUNT TITLES AND EXPLANATIONS	POST. REF.	DEBIT	CREDIT

Exercise 16–16 ① ② ③ ⑤

After issuing bonds in Chapter 15, Lee Consulting Corporation has some excess cash on hand. Michael Lee, the corporation's major shareholder, intends to invest some of the cash for different time periods to get better returns than from the bank and to have cash available when needed to expand the business into a new market. Assume Lee Consulting Corporation completed the following investment transactions:

2017

Apr.	15	The business purchased 300 common shares of Canadian Tire Corporation, Limited for $114.00 per share. Michael Lee intends to hold this investment for less than a year. He thinks the share value will increase and knows Lee Consulting will need the cash for operations in less than a year. Assume there were no brokerage fees.
Jun.	2	Purchased 2,000 of the 6,000 common shares of Landers Consulting Ltd. at a cost of $40,000. Landers Consulting is a company formed by a colleague of Lee, so Lee hopes the investment will lead to future business opportunities for Lee Consulting.
	15	Purchased $10,000 of 6 percent, four-year bonds of Consulting Suppliers Inc. at 115. Lee intends to hold these to maturity since the effective interest rate is still better than other investments he assessed.
Jul.	1	Received the quarterly cash dividend of $0.55 per share on the Canadian Tire investment.
Dec.	10	Received an annual dividend of $0.50 per share from Landers Consulting Ltd. Also received word that at November 30, Landers' year end, net income was $60,000.
	15	Received semi-annual interest of $300 on the Consulting Suppliers Inc. bonds. Amortized the premium using the straight-line method.

Required

1. Record the transactions in the general journal of Lee Consulting Corporation. Disregard any commissions on purchases and sales of investments.

2. Post entries to the Investment in Landers Consulting Ltd. Common Shares T-account. Determine its balance at December 10, 2017, after the transaction shown on that date.

Requirement 1

General Journal

DATE		ACCOUNT TITLES AND EXPLANATIONS	POST. REF.	DEBIT	CREDIT

Requirement 1 (Continued)

General Journal

DATE		ACCOUNT TITLES AND EXPLANATIONS	POST. REF.	DEBIT	CREDIT

Requirement 2

Investment in Landers Consulting Ltd. Common Shares

Problem 16–1A ① ② ③

Oliver Corp. owns numerous investments in the shares of other companies. Assume Oliver Corp. completed the following investment transactions:

2017

May	1	Purchased 12,000 common shares (total issued and outstanding common shares, 50,000) of Larson Corp. at a cost of $950,000. Commissions on the purchase were $20,000.
Jul.	2	Purchased 2,000 Larson Corp. common shares at a cost of $162,000. Commissions on the purchase were $1,500.
Sep.	15	Received semi-annual cash dividend of $3.20 per share on the Larson Corp. investment.
Oct.	12	Purchased 1,000 Sharma Ltd. common shares as a short-term investment, paying $33.00 per share plus brokerage commission of $1,000.
Dec.	14	Received semi-annual cash dividend of $1.50 per share on the Sharma Ltd. investment.
	31	Received annual report from Larson Corp. Net income for the year was $800,000. Of this amount, Oliver Corp.'s proportion is 28 percent. The current market value for 1,000 Sharma Ltd. shares is $31,000.

2018

Feb.	6	Sold 2,000 Larson Corp. shares for cash of $168,500, less commissions of $1,550.

Required   Record the transactions in the general journal of Oliver Corp.; the company's year end is December 31.

General Journal					
DATE		ACCOUNT TITLES AND EXPLANATIONS	POST. REF.	DEBIT	CREDIT

General Journal

DATE	ACCOUNT TITLES AND EXPLANATIONS	POST. REF.	DEBIT	CREDIT

Problem 16-5A ④

On July 18, 2017, Patrone Holdings Ltd. paid $1,920,000 to purchase 90 percent of the common shares of Smirnoff Inc., and Smirnoff Inc. owes Patrone Holdings Ltd. $240,000 on a note payable. All historical cost amounts are equal to their fair market value on July 18, 2017. Immediately after the purchase, the two companies' balance sheets were as follows:

Required Prepare a consolidation worksheet.

	PATRONE HOLDINGS LTD.	SMIRNOFF INC.	ELIMINATION DEBIT	ELIMINATION CREDIT	CONSOLIDATED AMOUNTS
Assets					
Cash	200,000	340,000			
Accounts receivable, net	720,000	480,000			
Note receivable from Smirnoff Inc.	240,000	—			
Inventory	1,480,000	920,000			
Investment in Smirnoff Inc.	1,920,000	—			
Property, plant, and equipment, net	2,190,000	1,540,000			
Goodwill	—	—			
Total	6,750,000	3,280,000			
Liabilities and Shareholders' Equity					
Accounts payable	1,060,000	680,000			
Notes payable	1,680,000	320,000			
Note payable to Patrone Holdings Ltd.	—	240,000			
Other liabilities	260,000	384,000			
Non-controlling interest	—	—			
Common shares	1,540,000	1,060,000			
Retained earnings	2,210,000	596,000			
Total	6,750,000	3,280,000			

Problem 16–6A

Financial institutions such as insurance companies and pension plans hold large quantities of bond investments. Suppose Sun Life Insurance Company purchases $1,000,000 of 3.00 percent bonds of Hydro-Québec at 102.00 on July 1, 2017. These bonds pay interest on January 1 and July 1 each year. They mature on July 1, 2037. At December 31, 2017, the market price of the bonds is 101.00. Sun Life plans to hold these bonds to maturity. Disregard commissions.

Required

1. Journalize Sun Life's purchase of the bonds as a long-term investment in bonds on July 1, 2017, and accrual of interest revenue and amortization of the discount for six months at December 31, 2017. Assume the straight-line method is appropriate for amortizing the discount.
2. Calculate the carrying value of the Hydro-Québec bonds at December 31, 2017.

Requirement 1

General Journal

DATE		ACCOUNT TITLES AND EXPLANATIONS	POST. REF.	DEBIT	CREDIT

Requirement 2

Problem 16–7A ⑤

On December 31, 2017, when the market interest rate is 6 percent, an investor purchases $700,000 of Solar Ltd. 10-year, 5 percent bonds at issuance for $647,929. Interest is paid semi-annually. Assume that the investor plans to hold the investment to maturity. Disregard commissions.

Required Prepare a schedule for amortizing the discount on the bond investment through December 31, 2018. The investor uses the effective-interest amortization method. Use Exhibit 15–5 on page 852 as a guide. Journalize the purchase on December 31, 2017, the first semi-annual interest receipt on June 30, 2018, and the year-end interest receipt on December 31, 2018.

SEMI-ANNUAL INTEREST PERIOD	A INTEREST RECEIPT (% OF MATURITY VALUES)	B INTEREST REVENUE (% OF PRECEDING INVESTMENT CARRYING AMOUNT)	C DISCOUNT AMORTIZATION (B - A)	D DISCOUNT ACCOUNT BALANCE (Previous D – Current C)	E INVESTMENT CARRYING AMOUNT (Investment – D)

General Journal

DATE	ACCOUNT TITLES AND EXPLANATIONS	POST. REF.	DEBIT	CREDIT

Problem 16–9A   ⑥

Global Networking Corporation completed the following transactions:

2017

Dec.	1	Sold machinery on account to a Japanese company for $45,000. The exchange rate of the Japanese yen is $0.0113, and the Japanese company agrees to pay in Canadian dollars.
	10	Purchased supplies on account from a US company at a price of US$125,000. The exchange rate of the US dollar is $1.06, and payment will be in US dollars.
	17	Sold machinery on account to an English firm for 220,000 British pounds. Payment will be in pounds, and the exchange rate of the pound is $1.61.
	22	Collected from the Japanese company. The exchange rate of the yen has not changed since December 1.
	31	Adjusted the accounts for changes in foreign-currency exchange rates. Current rates: US dollar, $1.10; British pound, $1.59.

2018

Jan.	18	Paid the US company. The exchange rate of the US dollar is $1.08.
	24	Collected from the English firm. The exchange rate of the British pound is $1.63.

Required

1. Record these transactions in Global Networking Corporation's general journal, and show how to report the transaction gain or loss on the income statement for the fiscal year ended December 31, 2017. For simplicity, use Sales Revenue as the credit.

2. How will what you have learned in this problem help you structure international transactions?

Requirement 1

General Journal

DATE	ACCOUNT TITLES AND EXPLANATIONS	POST. REF.	DEBIT	CREDIT

Requirement 1 (Continued)

General Journal

DATE		ACCOUNT TITLES AND EXPLANATIONS	POST. REF.	DEBIT	CREDIT

Requirement 2

17 THE CASH FLOW STATEMENT

LEARNING OBJECTIVES

1 Identify the purposes of the cash flow statement.
2 Identify cash flows from operating, investing, and financing activities.
3 Prepare a cash flow statement by the direct method.
4 Compute the cash effects of a wide variety of business transactions.
5 Prepare a cash flow statement by the indirect method.
6 Identify the impact of IFRS on the cash flow statement.

Starter 17–3 ①

Which company shown below is likely a startup company rather than an established company? Give reasons for your answer.

	Company X	Company Y
Cash inflow (outflow)—operating activities	$ (10,000)	$50,000
Cash inflow (outflow)—investing activities	(100,000)	30,000
Cash inflow (outflow)—financing activities	80,000	(20,000)
Income (loss) for the year	20,000	20,000

_____

_____

_____

_____

_____

_____

_____

_____

_____

Starter 17–4 ②

Latham Company expects the following for 2017:
- Net cash provided by operating activities of $120,000
- Net cash provided by financing activities of $48,000
- Net cash used for investing activities of $64,000 (no sales of long-term assets)

How much free cash flow does Latham Company expect for 2017?

_____

_____

_____

_____

_____

_____

_____

_____

_____

Starter 17–5 ③

Memmot Health Labs Inc. began 2017 with cash of $65,000. During the year, Memmot earned service revenue of $650,000 and collected $660,000 from customers. Expenses for the year totalled $470,000, of which Memmot paid $460,000 in cash to suppliers and employees. Memmot also paid $150,000 to purchase equipment and paid a cash dividend of $40,000 to its shareholders during 2017.

Prepare the company's cash flow statement for the year ended December 31, 2017. Format operating activities by the direct method.

Starter 17–9 ③ ④

Techno Toys Ltd. had the following comparative balance sheet:

TECHNO TOYS LTD.					
Balance Sheet					
December 31, 2017 and 2016					
Assets	**2017**	**2016**	**Liabilities**	**2017**	**2016**
Current			Current		
Cash	$ 57,000	$ 48,000	Accounts payable	$ 141,000	$ 126,000
Accounts receivable	162,000	144,000	Salary payable	69,000	63,000
Inventory	240,000	232,000	Accrued liabilities	24,000	33,000
Prepaid expenses	9,000	6,000	Long-term notes payable	198,000	204,000
Long-term investments	225,000	270,000	**Shareholders' Equity**		
Property and equipment, net	675,000	575,000	Common shares	120,000	111,000
			Retained earnings	816,000	738,000
Total	$1,368,000	$1,275,000	Total	$1,368,000	$1,275,000

Compute the following for Techno Toys Ltd.:

a. Collections from customers during 2017. Sales totalled $420,000.

b. Payments for inventory during 2017, assuming the change in Accounts Payable is due to inventory. Cost of goods sold was $240,000.

a. Collections from customers:

Accounts Receivable

b. Payments for inventory

Inventory　　　　　　　　　　　Accounts Payable

Starter 17–13 ⑤

Urgent Printers reported the following data for 2017:

Income Statement	
Net income	$63,000
Amortization expense	10,000
Balance sheet	
Increase in Accounts Receivable	7,000
Decrease in Accounts Payable	5,000

Compute Urgent Printers' net cash provided by operating activities using the indirect method.

Starter 17–17 ⑥

1. Under IFRS, what options does an entity have for classifying cash inflows from interest and dividends on the statement of cash flows? How does this differ from ASPE?

2. Under IFRS, what options does an entity have for classifying cash payments of interest and dividends on the statement of cash flows? How does this differ from ASPE?

_____

_____

_____

_____

_____

_____

_____

_____

_____

_____

_____

Exercise 17–3 ②

Identify each of the following transactions as an operating activity (O), an investing activity (I), a financing activity (F), a non-cash investing and financing activity (NIF), or a transaction that is not reported on the cash flow statement (N). For each cash flow, indicate whether the item increases (+) or decreases (–) cash. Assume the *indirect* method is used to report cash flows from operating activities.

Activity	(+)/(–)	Transactions
a.	_____	Amortization of equipment
b.	_____	Sale of long-term investment at a loss
c.	_____	Payment of cash dividend
d.	_____	Increase in inventory
e.	_____	Issuance of preferred shares for cash
f.	_____	Prepaid expenses decreased during the year
g.	_____	Accrual of salaries expense
h.	_____	Issuance of long-term note payable to borrow cash
i.	_____	Cash sale of land
j.	_____	Payment of long-term debt

Exercise 17–4 ②

Consider three independent cases for the cash flow data of Rennie Recreation Products Inc.:

	Case A	Case B	Case C
Cash flows from operating activities:			
Net income	$ 120,000	$ 12,000	$ 120,000
Amortization	44,000	44,000	44,000
Increase in current assets	(4,000)	(28,000)	(76,000)
Decrease in current liabilities	0	(32,000)	(24,000)
	160,000	(4,000)	64,000
Cash flows from investing activities:			
Acquisition of property, plant, and equipment	$(364,000)	$(364,000)	$(364,000)
Sales of property, plant, and equipment	16,000	16,000	388,000
	(348,000)	(348,000)	24,000
Cash flows from financing activities:			
New borrowing	200,000	516,000	64,000
Payment of debt	(36,000)	(116,000)	(84,000)
	164,000	400,000	(20,000)
Net increase (decrease) in cash	$ (24,000)	$ 48,000	$ 68,000

Required For each case, identify from the cash flow statement the primary method that Rennie Recreation Products Inc. used to generate the cash to acquire new property, plant, and equipment.

Cases A – C

_____

_____

_____

_____

_____

_____

_____

_____

_____

_____

_____

_____

_____

_____

_____

_____

Exercise 17–9 ③

The accounting records of Koltire Auto Parts Ltd. reveal the following:

Acquisition of land	$ 89,000	Loss on sale of land	$ 6,000
Amortization	50,000	Net income	78,000
Cash sales	78,000	Payment of accounts payable	110,000
Collection of accounts receivable	186,000	Payment of dividends	25,000
Collection of dividend revenue	4,000	Payment of income tax	8,000
Decrease in current liabilities	52,000	Payment of interest	14,000
Increase in current assets other than cash	48,000	Payment of salaries and wages	76,000

Required   Compute cash flows from operating activities by the direct method. Use the format of the operating activities section of Exhibit 17–14.

Exercise 17–11 ② ③

The income statement and additional data of Flashpoint Consulting Ltd. follow:

FLASHPOINT CONSULTING LTD.		
Income Statement		
For the Year Ended September 30, 2017		
Revenues		
Consulting revenue		$548,000
Expenses		
Salaries expense	$296,000	
Amortization expense	58,000	
Rent expense	14,000	
Office supplies expense	16,000	
Insurance expense	4,000	
Interest expense	4,000	
Income tax expense	36,000	428,000
Net income		$120,000

Additional data:

a. Collections from clients were $114,000 more than revenues.

b. Increase in cash balance, $20,000.

c. Payments to employees are $8,000 less than salaries expense.

d. Interest expense and income tax expense equal their cash amounts.

e. Acquisition of computer equipment is $232,000. Of this amount, $202,000 was paid in cash and $30,000 by signing a long-term note payable.

f. Cash received from sale of land, $20,000.

g. Cash received from issuance of common shares, $84,000.

h. Payment of long-term note payable, $40,000.

i. Payment of cash dividends, $130,000.

j. Payments for rent and insurance were equal to expense.

k. Payment for office supplies was $12,000 more than expense.

Prepare Flashpoint Consulting Ltd.'s cash flow statement by the direct method and the note to the financial statements giving the summary of non-cash investing and financing activities. Evaluate Flashpoint's cash flow for the year. Mention all three categories of cash flows and the reason for your evaluation.

Exercise 17-17 ⑤

Repage Inc. reported a net cash flow from operating activities of $40,625 on its cash flow statement for the year ended December 31, 2017. The following information was reported in the Cash Flows from Operating Activities section of the cash flow statement, which uses the *indirect* method:

Decrease in legal fees payable	$1,000
Increase in prepaid expenses	400
Amortization	3,350
Loss on sale of equipment	1,500
Increase in accounts payable	600
Decrease in inventories	2,175
Increase in trade accounts receivable	2,000

Required Determine the net income reported by Repage Inc. for the year ended December 31, 2017.

Hint: Prepare the Operating Activities section and solve for the net income figure.

Exercise 17–18   ⑤

The accounting records of Iberia Corporation reveal the following:

Acquisition of land	$ 444,000	Increase in current assets other than cash	$252,000
Amortization	156,000	Loss on sale of land	60,000
Cash sales	108,000	Net income	288,000
Collection of accounts receivable	1,116,000	Payment of accounts payable	576,000
Collection of dividend revenue	108,000	Payment of dividends	84,000
Decrease in current liabilities	276,000	Payment of income tax	96,000
		Payment of interest	192,000
		Payment of salaries and wages	432,000

Compute cash flows from operating activities by the indirect method. Use the format of the operating activities section of Exhibit 17–16. Then evaluate Iberia Corporation's operating cash flows as strong or weak (omit the date from the statement heading).

Exercise 17–21 ② ⑤

Prepare the 2017 cash flow statement for Valemont Corporation using the indirect method to report cash flows from operating activities.

Transaction data for 2017

Amortization expense	$ 40,000	Payment of cash dividends	$ 72,000
Issuance of long-term note payable to borrow cash	28,000	Net income	104,000
Issuance of common shares for cash	76,000	Purchase of long-term investment	32,000
Cash received from sale of building	296,000	Issuance of long-term note payable to purchase patent	148,000
Repurchase of own shares	20,000	Issuance of common shares to retire $52,000 of bonds	52,000
Loss on sale of building	8,000		
Purchase of equipment	392,000		

	December 31,		
	2017	**2016**	
Current assets			
Cash and cash equivalents	$ 76,000	$ 12,000	
Accounts receivable	88,000	92,000	
Inventories	136,000	124,000	
Prepaid expenses	4,000	12,000	
Current liabilities			
Notes payable (for inventory purchases)	$ 44,000	$ 28,000	
Accounts payable	96,000	76,000	
Accrued liabilities	28,000	36,000	
Income and other taxes payable	40,000	40,000	

Exercise 17–22 ② ⑤ ⑥

The income statement and additional data of Wandell Consulting Ltd. follow:

WANDELL CONSULTING LTD.		
Income Statement		
For the Year Ended December 31, 2017		
Revenues:		
Consulting revenue		$137,000
Expenses:		
Salaries expense	$74,000	
Amortization expense	14,500	
Rent expense	6,000	
Office supplies expense	1,500	
Insurance expense	1,000	
Interest expense	1,000	
Income tax expense	9,000	107,000
Net income		$30,000

Additional data:

a. Collections from clients are $3,500 more than revenues.

b. Increase in cash balance, $5,000.

c. Payments to employees are $2,000 less than salaries expense.

d. Interest expense and income tax expense equal their cash amounts.

e. Acquisition of property, plant, and equipment is $58,000. Of this amount, $50,500 is paid in cash, $7,500 by signing a long-term note payable.

f. Cash received from sale of land, $5,000.

g. Cash received from issuance of common shares, $21,000.

h. Payment of long-term note payable, $10,000.

i. Payment of cash dividends, $7,500.

j. Payments for rent and insurance are equal to expense.

k. Payment for office supplies is $3,000 more than expense.

l. Opening cash balance, $8,000.

Required

1. Prepare Wandell Consulting Ltd.'s cash flow statement by the direct method for operating activities and a note to the financial statements providing a summary of non-cash investing and financing activities.

2. Assume Wandell Consulting Ltd. has adopted IFRS. What would be the difference in the cash flow statement using this framework?

Requirement 1

Requirement 2

Exercise 17–23 ② ⑤

Suppose, at December 31, 2017, Lee Consulting Corporation has the following comparative balance sheet:

LEE CONSULTING CORPORATION		
Balance Sheet		
December 31, 2017 and 2016		
	2017	**2016**
Current assets		
Cash	$ 5,000	$ 8,100
Accounts receivable	2,200	1,700
Supplies	420	300
Equipment	10,000	2,000
Furniture	3,600	3,600
Building	55,000	—
Less: accumulated amortization	(2,753)	(93)
Land	20,000	—
Total assets	$93,467	$15,607
Current liabilities		
Accounts payable	$ 350	$ 3,900
Salary payable	2,500	—
Long-term liabilities		
Notes payable	40,000	—
Shareholders' equity		
Common shares	20,000	10,000
Retained earnings	30,617	1,707
Total liabilities and shareholders' equity	$93,467	$15,607

Additional information: Lee Consulting Corporation declared and paid $10,000 in dividends during 2017. Net income for the year ended December 31, 2017, was $38,910.

Required   Using this information, prepare the cash flow statement for Lee Consulting Corporation using the indirect method for operating activities.

Problem 17–2A ② ③

Sawyer Products Ltd.'s accountants have developed the following data from the company's accounting records for the year ended July 31, 2017:

a. Salaries expense, $631,800.

b. Cash payments to purchase property, plant, and equipment, $1,035,000.

c. Proceeds from issuance of long-term debt, $264,600.

d. Payments of long-term debt, $142,800.

e. Proceeds from sale of property, plant, and equipment, $318,200.

f. Interest revenue, $72,600.

g. Cash receipt of dividend revenue on investments in shares, $56,200.

h. Payments to suppliers, $4,129,800.

i. Interest expense and payments, $226,800.

j. Cost of goods sold, $2,886,600.

k. Collection of interest revenue, $30,200.

l. Acquisition of equipment by issuing short-term note payable, $213,000.

m. Payment of salaries, $804,000.

n. Credit sales, $3,648,600.

o. Income tax expense and payments, $338,400.

p. Amortization expense, $309,600.

q. Collections on accounts receivable, $4,038,600.

r. Collection of long-term notes receivable, $486,400.

s. Proceeds from sale of investments, $538,200.

t. Payment of long-term debt by issuing common shares, $900,000.

u. Cash sales, $1,134,000.

v. Proceeds from issuance of common shares, $589,400.

w. Payment of cash dividends, $310,000.

x. Cash balance:

July 31, 2016—$654,800

July 31, 2017—$?

Required

1. Prepare Sawyer Products Ltd.'s cash flow statement for the year ended July 31, 2017, using the direct method for the operating activities section. Follow the format of Exhibit 17–14, but do *not* show amounts in thousands. Include a note to the financial statements giving a summary of non-cash investing and financing activities.

2. Evaluate 2017 in terms of cash flow. Give your reasons.

Requirement 1

Requirement 1 (Continued)

Requirement 2

Problem 17–3A ② ③ ④

The 2017 comparative balance sheet and income statement of Whitbey Group Inc. follow:

WHITBEY GROUP INC.		
Balance Sheet		
August 31, 2017 and 2016		
	2017	2016
Current assets		
Cash and cash equivalents	$ 47,000	$ 156,000
Accounts receivable	415,000	431,000
Interest receivable	6,000	9,000
Inventories	993,000	899,000
Prepaid expenses	17,000	22,000
Plant and equipment, net	1,009,000	937,000
Land	401,000	200,000
Total assets	$2,888,000	$2,654,000
Current liabilities		
Accounts payable	$ 114,000	$ 179,000
Interest payable	63,000	67,000
Wages payable	71,000	14,000
Lease liabilities	181,000	187,000
Income tax payable	73,000	38,000
Long-term liabilities		
Notes payable	450,000	650,000
Shareholders' equity		
Common shares	1,411,000	1,223,000
Retained earnings	525,000	296,000
Total liabilities and shareholders' equity	$2,888,000	$2,654,000

WHITBEY GROUP INC.		
Income Statement		
For the Year Ended August 31, 2017		
Revenues:		
Sales revenue		$4,380,000
Interest revenue		17,000
Total revenues		4,397,000
Expenses:		
Cost of goods sold	$1,952,000	
Salaries expense	814,000	
Amortization expense	253,000	
Other operating expenses*	497,000	
Interest expense	246,000	
Income tax expense	169,000	
Total expenses		3,931,000
Net income		$ 466,000

*Includes lease liability and prepaid expense.

Whitbey Group had no non-cash investing and financing transactions during 2017. During the year, there were no sales of land or plant and equipment, no issuances of notes payable, and no repurchase of common shares.

Required

1. Prepare the 2017 cash flow statement, formatting operating activities by the direct method.
2. Evaluate the 2017 cash flow for this company.

Requirement 1

Calculations:

Requirement 2

_____
_____
_____
_____
_____
_____
_____
_____
_____
_____
_____
_____
_____
_____
_____
_____

Problem 17–5A ② ⑤

Accountants for Natures Design Ltd. have assembled the following data for the year ended December 31, 2017:

	December 31,		
	2017	2016	
Current accounts (all result from operations)			
Current assets			
Cash and cash equivalents	$ 9,050	$ 8,700	
Accounts receivable	17,025	18,425	
Inventories	29,625	24,125	
Prepaid expenses	800	525	
Current liabilities			
Notes payable (for inventory purchases)	7,575	9,200	
Accounts payable	18,025	16,875	
Income tax payable	1,475	1,950	
Accrued liabilities	12,075	5,800	

Transaction data for 2017:

Acquisition of building by issuing		Issuance of common shares, class B, for cash	$14,050	
long-term note payable	$33,000	Net income	12,625	
Acquisition of farm equipment	18,500	Payment of cash dividends	10,700	
Acquisition of long-term investment	11,200	Payment of long-term debt	16,950	
Amortization expense	5,075	Retirement of bonds		
Collection of loan	2,575	payable by issuing preferred shares	22,350	
Gain on sale of investment	875	Sale of long-term investment for cash	5,550	
Issuance of long-term debt to borrow cash	17,750	Share dividends	10,150	

Required

1. Prepare Natures Design Ltd.'s cash flow statement using the *indirect* method to report operating activities. Include a note regarding non-cash investing and financing activities.

2. Evaluate Natures Design Ltd.'s cash flows for the year. Mention all three categories of cash flows, and give the reason for your evaluation.

Requirement 1

Calculations:

Requirement 2

Problem 17–6A ② ③ ④ ⑤

To prepare the cash flow statement, accountants for Fothingham Sales Ltd. have summarized 2017 activity in two T-accounts as follows:

Cash

Beginning balance	87,100	Payments of operating expenses	46,100
Sale of common shares	80,800	Payment of long-term debt	78,900
Receipts of dividends	17,900	Repurchase of common shares	30,400
Sale of investments	28,400	Payment of income tax	6,000
Receipts of interest	22,200	Payments on accounts payable	101,600
Collections from customers	307,000	Payments of dividends	16,000
		Payments of salaries and wages	67,500
		Payments of interest	41,800
		Purchase of equipment	79,900
Ending balance	75,200		

Common Shares

Repurchase of common shares	30,400	Beginning balance	103,500
		Issuance for cash	80,800
		Issuance to acquire land	64,500
		Issuance to retire long-term debt	31,600
		Ending balance	250,000

Fothingham Sales Ltd.'s 2017 income statement and selected balance sheet data follow:

FOTHINGHAM SALES LTD.		
Income Statement		
For the Year Ended October 31, 2017		
Revenues and gains:		
Sales revenue		$317,000
Interest revenue		22,200
Dividend revenue		17,900
Gain on sale of investments		700
Total revenues and gains		357,800
Expenses:		
Cost of goods sold	$103,600	
Salaries and wages expense	66,800	
Amortization expense	10,900	
Other operating expenses	44,700	
Interest expense	44,100	
Income tax expense	9,200	
Total expenses		279,300
Net income		$ 78,500

FOTHINGHAM SALES LTD.	
Balance Sheet Data	
For the Year Ended October 31, 2017	
	Increase (Decrease)
Current assets	
Cash and cash equivalents	$?
Accounts receivable	10,000
Inventories	5,700
Prepaid expenses	(1,900)
Investments	(27,700)
Plant and equipment, net	69,000
Land	75,000
Current liabilities	
Accounts payable	7,700
Interest payable	2,300
Salaries payable	(700)
Other accrued liabilities	(3,300)
Income tax payable	3,200
Long-term debt	(100,000)
Common shares	146,500
Retained earnings	62,500

Required

1. Prepare Fothingham Sales Ltd.'s cash flow statement for the year ended October 31, 2017, using the *direct* method to report operating activities. Also prepare a note to the financial statements summarizing the non-cash investing and financing activities.

2. Prepare a schedule showing cash flows from operating activities using the *indirect* method. All activity in the current accounts results from operations.

Requirement 1

Requirement 1 (Continued)

Note to financial statements:	

Requirement 2

Problem 17–8A ② ④ ⑤

The financial statements for Facetime Corp. for the year ended December 31, 2017, are as follows:

FACETIME CORP.			
Balance Sheet			
December 31, 2017 and 2016			
	2017	2016	
Assets			
Cash	$ 10,000	$ 18,000	
Investment in money market fund	0	40,000	
Accounts receivable	189,000	175,000	
Merchandise inventory	280,000	610,000	
Prepaid expenses	30,000	23,000	
Plant and equipment	1,798,000	1,654,000	
Less accumulated amortization	(160,000)	(120,000)	
Investment	200,000	0	
Goodwill	90,000	100,000	
Total assets	$2,437,000	$2,500,000	
Liabilities			
Accounts payable	$ 176,000	$ 120,000	
Salaries payable	110,000	100,000	
Loan payable	350,000	400,000	
Total liabilities	636,000	620,000	
Shareholders' equity			
Preferred shares	800,000	500,000	
Common shares	500,000	500,000	
Retained earnings	501,000	880,000	
Total shareholders' equity	1,801,000	1,880,000	
Total liabilities and shareholders' equity	$2,437,000	$2,500,000	

FACETIME CORP.		
Income Statement		
For the Year Ended December 31, 2017		
Net sales		$1,600,000
Cost of goods sold		840,000
Gross margin		760,000
Operating expenses:		
Selling expenses	350,000	
Administrative expenses	230,000	
Interest expense	40,000	
Total operating expenses		620,000
Operating income		140,000
Income taxes		39,000
Net income		$ 101,000

Additional information:

a. The administrative expenses included the following:

Amortization expense on plant and equipment, $100,000.

Write-down of goodwill, $10,000.

b. Sold equipment for its book value. The equipment cost $430,000 and had been amortized for $60,000.

c. Purchased additional equipment in December for $574,000.

d. Issued preferred shares for an investment purchase of $200,000.

e. Declared and paid cash dividends: preferred, $230,000; common, $250,000.

f. Sold 20,000 preferred shares for $5.00 per share.

g. Paid $90,000 (of which $40,000 was interest) on the loans.

Required

1. Prepare a cash flow statement for Facetime Corp. for the year ended December 31, 2017, using the *indirect* method. The investment in the money market fund is a cash equivalent.

2. Did the company improve its cash position in 2017? Give your reasons.

Requirement 1

Requirement 2

18 FINANCIAL STATEMENT ANALYSIS

LEARNING OBJECTIVES

1 Perform a horizontal analysis of financial statements.
2 Perform a vertical analysis of financial statements.
3 Prepare and use common-size financial statements.
4 Compute the standard financial ratios.
5 Describe the impact of IFRS on financial statement analysis.

Starter 18–6 ① ② ④

Match each of the following terms with its description. Place the letter for the description in the blank beside the term.

Terms	Description
_____ 1. Horizontal analysis	a. Ability to meet current payments as they come due.
_____ 2. Quick ratio	b. Ratio of cost of goods sold to average inventory.
_____ 3. Vertical analysis	c. Ratio of total liabilities to total assets.
_____ 4. Debt ratio	d. Ratio of the sum of cash plus short-term investments plus net current receivables to current liabilities.
_____ 5. Inventory turnover	e. Analysis of a financial statement that reveals the relationship of each statement item to a total, which is 100 percent.
_____ 6. Liquidity	f. Earning more income on borrowed money than the related expense, thereby increasing the earnings for the owners of the business.
_____ 7. Leverage	g. The use of percentage changes in comparative financial statements.

Use the following data for Starters 18–8 through 18–12. Jeryht Bakers Corp., a baking-supplies chain, reported these summarized figures (in millions):

JERYHT BAKERS CORP.	
Income Statement	
For the Year Ended December 31, 2017	
Net sales	$61.6
Cost of goods sold	42.4
Interest expense	0.6
All other expenses	15.0
Net income	$ 3.6

JERYHT BAKERS CORP.					
Balance Sheet					
December 31					
	2017	**2016**		**2017**	**2016**
Cash	$ 2.8	$ 1.6	Total current liabilities	$ 8.8	$ 7.2
Short-term investments	0.4	0.5	Long-term liabilities	8.6	8.3
Accounts receivable	0.5	0.4	Total liabilities	17.4	15.5
Inventory	9.2	8.0	Common shares	5.2	4.8
Other current assets	0.8	0.6	Retained earnings	15.7	11.8
Total current assets	13.7	11.1	Total equity	20.9	16.6
All other assets	24.6	21.0	Total liabilities and equity	$38.3	$32.1
Total assets	$38.3	$32.1			

Starter 18–8 ④

Use the Jeryht Bakers Corp. balance sheet data given above.

1. Compute the company's current ratio at December 31, 2017 and 2016.
2. Did Jeryht Bakers Corp.'s current ratio value improve, deteriorate, or hold steady during 2017?

1. Current ratio   2017   2016

2. _____
   _____
   _____
   _____
   _____

Starter 18–9 ④

Use the Jeryht Bakers Corp. data to compute the following (amounts in millions):

a. The rate of inventory turnover for 2017.
b. Days' sales in receivables during 2017. All sales are made on account. Round dollar amounts to three decimal places.

a. Inventory turnover:

b. Days' sales in receivables:

Starter 18–10 ④

Use the financial statements of Jeryht Bakers Corp.

1. Compute the debt ratio at December 31, 2017.
2. Is Jeryht Bakers Corp.'s ability to pay its liabilities strong or weak? Explain your reasoning.

1. Debt ratio:

2. _____
   _____
   _____
   _____
   _____
   _____

Starter 18–11 ④

Use the financial statements of Jeryht Bakers Corp.

1. Compute these profitability measures for 2017:
   a. Rate of return on net sales
   b. Rate of return on total assets; interest expense for 2017 was $0.6 million
   c. Rate of return on common shareholders' equity
2. Are these rates of return strong or weak? Explain.

1. a. Rate of return on net sales:

   b. Rate of return on total assets:

   c. Rate of return on common shareholders' equity:

2. _____
_____
_____
_____
_____
_____

Starter 18–12 ④

Use the financial statements of Jeryht Bakers Corp., plus the following item (in millions):

Number of common shares outstanding 0.8

1. Compute earnings per share (EPS) for Jeryht Bakers Corp. Round to the nearest cent.
2. Compute Jeryht Bakers Corp.'s price–earnings ratio. The price of a Jeryht Bakers Corp. common share is $131.00.

1. EPS:

2. Price/earnings ratio:

Starter 18–13 ④

A summary of Pasmore Ltd.'s income statement appears as follows:

PASMORE LTD.	
Income Statement	
For the Year Ended March 31, 2016	
Net sales	$3,600
Cost of goods sold	(A)
Selling and administrative expenses	855
Interest expenses	(B)
Other expenses	75
Income before taxes	500
Income tax expenses	(C)
Net income	$ (D)

Use the following ratio data to complete Pasmore Ltd.'s income statement:

a. Inventory turnover was 5.50 (beginning inventory was $395, ending inventory was $375).

b. Rate of return on sales is 0.095, or 9.5 percent.

Calculations:

Starter 18–14 ④

A summary of Pasmore Ltd.'s balance sheet appears as follows:

PASMORE LTD.			
Balance Sheet			
March 31, 2016			
Cash	$ 25	Total current liabilities	$1,050
Receivables	(A)	Long-term note payable	(E)
Inventories	375	Other long-term liabilities	410
Prepaid expenses	(B)		
Total current assets	(C)		
Property, plant, and equipment, net	(D)		
Other assets	1,075	Shareholders' equity	1,200
Total assets	$3,400	Total liabilities and equity	$ (F)

Use the following ratio data to complete Pasmore Ltd.'s balance sheet:

a. Current ratio is 0.70.

b. Acid-test ratio is 0.30.

Exercise 18–1 ①

Compute the dollar change and the percentage change in Navin Ltd.'s working capital each year during 2016 and 2017. Is this trend favourable or unfavourable?

NAVIN LTD.			
	2017	**2016**	**2015**
Total current assets	$92,250	$87,000	$78,750
Total current liabilities	37,200	34,750	42,500

_____

_____

_____

_____

_____

Exercise 18–2 ①

Prepare a horizontal analysis of the comparative income statement of Keesha Shoes Inc. Round percentage changes to the nearest one-tenth percent (three decimal places).

Why was the percentage increase in net income higher than that in total revenue during 2017?

KEESHA SHOES INC.				
Horizontal Analysis of Comparative Income Statement				
For the Years Ended December 31, 2017 and 2016				
			INCREASE (DECREASE)	
	2017	2016	AMOUNT	PERCENT
Net sales	$533,000	$465,000		
Expenses:				
Cost of goods sold	235,000	202,000		
Selling and general expenses	140,000	135,000		
Interest expense	10,000	6,000		
Wages expense	51,000	41,000		
Total expenses	436,000	384,000		
Net income	$ 97,000	$ 81,000		

Exercise 18–3   ①

Compute trend percentages for Ceder Inc.'s net sales and net income for the following five-year period, using 2013 as the base year:

	2017	2016	2015	2014	2013
			(Amounts in thousands)		
Net sales	$1,625	$1,469	$1,375	$1,200	$1,304
Net income	149	131	100	82	105

Which measure grew more during the period: net sales or net income? By what percentage did net sales and net income grow from 2013 to 2017?

Exercise 18–4 ②

Purposeful Products Inc. has requested that you perform a vertical analysis of its balance sheet. Determine the component percentages of its assets, liabilities, and shareholders' equity.

PURPOSEFUL PRODUCTS INC.		
Vertical Analysis of Balance Sheet		
December 31, 2017		
	AMOUNT	PERCENT
Assets		
Total current assets	$219,000	
Property, plant, and equipment, net	267,000	
Other assets	40,000	
Total assets	$526,000	
Liabilities		
Total current liabilities	$ 85,000	
Long-term debt	156,000	
Total liabilities	241,000	
Shareholders' Equity		
Total shareholders' equity	285,000	
Total liabilities and shareholders' equity	$526,000	

Exercise 18–6 ③

Prepare a common-size analysis to compare the asset composition of Bhagwan Inc. and Bigwig Ltd. (amounts in millions).
To which company are *current assets* more important? Which company places more emphasis on its *property, plant, and equipment*?

(Amounts in millions) ASSETS	BHAGWAN INC. AMOUNT	PERCENT	BIGWIG LTD. AMOUNT	PERCENT
Current assets:				
Cash and equivalents	$ 462		$ 472	
Short-term investments	—		804	
Accounts receivable, net	2,898		882	
Inventories	2,082		5,380	
Other current assets	408		134	
Total current assets	5,850		7,672	
Property, plant, and equipment, net	4,960		11,280	
Goodwill and other intangibles	206		226	
Other assets	302		540	
Total assets	$11,318		$19,718	

_____

_____

_____

Exercise 18–7 ④

Compare the results of two years of ratios for Prince George Corp.

Ratio	2017	2016	Change + or −	Benchmark	Performance + or −
Current ratio	1.5	1.7		2:1	
Acid-test ratio	0.83	0.85		0.95	
Inventory turnover	8	7		10	
Accounts receivable turnover	12	14		13	
Debt ratio	0.3	0.2		0.7	
Times-interest-earned ratio	7	6		4	
Rate of return on total assets	0.06	0.04		0.05	
Rate of return on common shareholders' equity	0.24	0.23		0.14	

Required

1. Identify whether the change from 2016 to 2017 was good (+) or bad (−).

2. Assess whether the performance in 2017 is good (+) or bad (−) compared with the industry average presented in the benchmark column.

Exercise 18–13   ④

Suppose at January 31, 2018, Lee Consulting Corporation has the following balance sheet:

LEE CONSULTING CORPORATION	
Balance Sheet	
January 31, 2018	
Assets	
Current assets:	
Cash	$ 5,000
Accounts receivable	2,200
Supplies	420
Total current assets	7,620
Equipment, net	15,150
Furniture, net	3,650
Building, net	52,227
Land	40,000
Total assets	$118,467
Liabilities and Shareholders' Equity	
Current liabilities:	
Accounts payable	$ 350
Salary payable	2,500
Total current liabilities	2,850
Long-term liabilities:	
Notes payable	40,000
Shareholders' equity:	
Common shares	45,000
Retained earnings	30,617
Total liabilities and shareholders' equity	$118,467

Additional information: Lee Consulting Corporation incurred interest expense of $2,400 during January. Net income for the month ended January 31, 2018, was $38,910. The market price of Lee Consulting Corporation's 1,500 common shares is $50.00 per share on January 31, 2018. Total shareholders' equity last year was $51,334.

Required   Using this information, calculate the following ratios for Lee Consulting Corporation:

a. Current ratio

b. Debt ratio

c. Earnings per share

d. Price–earnings ratio

e. Rate of return on total assets

f. Rate of return on common shareholders' equity

Comment on each as to whether you feel the business is doing well or not and why you think so.

a. – f.

Problem 18–1A ① ④

Net sales, net income, and common shareholders' equity for Naturah Products Ltd. for a six-year period follow:

	2017	2016	2015	2014	2013	2012
			(Amounts in thousands)			
Net sales	$1,806	$1,757	$1,606	$1,704	$1,638	$1,588
Net income	144	120	89	126	100	96
Ending common shareholders' equity	940	860	772	684	628	600

Required

1. Compute trend percentages for 2013 through 2017, using 2012 as the base year. Round to the nearest whole percentage.
2. Compute the rate of return on common shareholders' equity for 2013 through 2017, rounding to three decimal places. In this industry, rates of 12 percent are average, rates above 15 percent are considered good, and rates above 20 percent are viewed as outstanding.
3. How does Naturah Products Ltd.'s return on common shareholders' equity compare with the industry's?

Requirement 1

NATURAH PRODUCTS LTD.						
Trend Percentages						
	2017	2016	2015	2014	2013	2012
Net sales						
Net income						
Ending common shareholders' equity						

Requirement 2

	2017	2016	2015	2014	2013
(A) Net income					
(B) Average common shareholders' equity					
ROE = A ÷ B					
ROE as a Percentage					

Requirement 3

_____

_____

_____

Problem 18–2A ②

The McConnell Department Stores, Inc. chief executive officer (CEO) has asked you to compare the company's profit performance and financial position with the averages for the industry. The CEO has given you the company's income statement and balance sheet, as well as the industry average data for retailers.

MCCONNELL DEPARTMENT STORES, INC.		
Income Statement Compared with Industry Average		
For the Year Ended December 31, 2017		
	McConnell	Industry Average
Net sales	$778,000	100.0%
Cost of goods sold	522,816	65.8
Gross margin	255,184	34.2
Operating expenses	161,046	19.7
Operating income	94,138	14.5
Other expenses	4,668	0.4
Net income	$ 89,470	14.1%

MCCONNELL DEPARTMENT STORES, INC.		
Balance Sheet Compared with Industry Average		
December 31, 2017		
	McConnell	Industry Average
Current assets	$325,440	70.9%
Property, plant, and equipment	120,960	23.6
Intangible assets, net	8,640	0.8
Other assets	24,960	4.7
Total assets	$480,000	100.0%
Current liabilities	$222,720	48.1%
Long-term liabilities	107,520	16.6
Total liabilities	330,240	64.7
Shareholders' equity	149,760	35.3
Total liabilities and shareholders' equity	$480,000	100.0%

Required

1. Prepare a vertical analysis for McConnell for both its income statement and balance sheet.
2. Compare the company's gross margin and profit margin ratios with the average for the industry. Comment on their investment in assets as well as their debt to assets compared with the industry information shown.

Requirement 1

MCCONNELL DEPARTMENT STORES, INC.		
Income Statement		
For the Year Ended December 31, 2017		
		Percent of Total
Net sales	$ 778,000	
Cost of goods sold	522,816	
Gross margin	255,184	
Operating expenses	161,046	
Operating income	94,138	
Other expenses	4,668	
Net income	$ 89,470	

MCCONNELL DEPARTMENT STORES, INC.		
Balance Sheet		
December 31, 2017		
		Percent of Total
Current assets	$ 325,440	
Property, plant, and equipment, net	120,960	
Intangible assets, net	8,640	
Other assets	24,960	
Total assets	$ 480,000	
Current liabilities	$ 222,720	
Long-term liabilities	107,520	
Total liabilities	330,240	
Shareholders' equity	149,760	
Total liabilities and shareholders' equity	$ 480,000	

Requirement 2

Problem 18–4A ④

Financial statement data of MKR Dealer Supplies Ltd. include the following items:

Cash	$ 68,000
Accounts receivable, net	97,500
Inventories	129,000
Prepaid expenses	6,000
Total assets	625,000
Short-term notes payable	39,000
Accounts payable	109,500
Accrued liabilities	27,000
Long-term liabilities	204,000
Net income	108,000
Number of common shares outstanding	40,000 shares

Required

1. Compute MKR Dealer Supplies Ltd.'s current ratio, debt ratio, and earnings per share.
2. Compute each of the three ratios after evaluating the effect of each transaction that follows. Consider each transaction *separately*.
   a. Purchased merchandise of $43,000 on account, debiting Inventory.
   b. Paid long-term liabilities, $40,000.
   c. Declared, but did not pay, a $60,000 cash dividend on common shares.
   d. Borrowed $50,000 on a long-term note payable.
   e. Issued 10,000 common shares at the beginning of the year, receiving cash of $140,000.
   f. Received cash on account, $29,000.
   g. Paid short-term notes payable, $25,000.

Requirement 1

CURRENT RATIO	DEBT RATIO	EARNINGS PER SHARE

Requirement 2

	CURRENT RATIO	DEBT RATIO	EARNINGS PER SHARE
a.			
b.			
c.			
d.			
e.			
f.			
g.			

Problem 18–5A ④

Comparative financial statement data of Old Tyme Candies Corp. appear below:

OLD TYME CANDIES CORP.		
Income Statement		
For the Years Ended December 31, 2017 and 2016		
	2017	2016
Net sales	$311,850	$297,000
Cost of goods sold	148,850	147,000
Gross margin	163,000	150,000
Operating expenses	79,250	77,000
Income from operations	83,750	73,000
Interest expense	12,500	14,000
Income before income tax	71,250	59,000
Income tax expense	17,850	14,600
Net income	$ 53,400	$ 44,400

OLD TYME CANDIES CORP.			
Balance Sheet			
December 31, 2017 and 2016			
(selected 2015 amounts given for computation of ratios)			
	2017	2016	2015
Current assets:			
Cash	$ 27,500	$ 25,000	
Current receivables, net	67,500	62,500	$ 52,500
Inventories	127,500	117,500	95,000
Prepaid expenses	5,000	4,000	
Total current assets	227,500	209,000	
Property, plant, and equipment, net	100,500	98,000	
Total assets	$328,000	$307,000	295,500
Total current liabilities	$ 93,000	$100,725	
Long-term liabilities	117,500	127,500	
Total liabilities	210,500	228,225	
Preferred shares, $1.25	5,000	5,000	
Common shares	50,000	37,500	17,500
Retained earnings	62,500	36,275	25,000
Total liabilities and shareholders' equity	$328,000	$307,000	

Other information:

- Market price of Old Tyme Candies Corp. common shares: $24.00 at December 31, 2017, and $12.00 at December 31, 2016.
- Common shares outstanding: 10,000 during 2017 and 7,500 during 2016. There are 1,000 preferred shares outstanding at December 31, 2017 and 2016.
- All sales are on credit.

Required

1. Compute the following ratios for 2017 and 2016:
   a. Current ratio
   b. Inventory turnover
   c. Accounts receivable turnover
   d. Times-interest-earned ratio
   e. Return on assets
   f. Return on common shareholders' equity
   g. Earnings per common share
   h. Price–earnings ratio
   i. Book value per common share at year end
2. Decide (a) whether Old Tyme Candies Corp.'s financial position improved or deteriorated during 2017, and (b) whether the investment attractiveness of its common shares appears to have increased or decreased.
3. How will what you have learned in this problem help you evaluate an investment?

Requirement 1

	2017	2016
a. **Current ratio:**		
b. **Inventory turnover:**		
c. **Accounts receivable turnover:**		
d. **Times-interest-earned ratio:**		

Requirement 1 (Continued)

	2017	2016

e. Return on assets:

f. Return on common shareholders' equity:

g. Earnings per common share:

h. Price-earnings ratio:

i. Book value per common share at year end:

Requirements 2 & 3

_____
_____
_____
_____
_____
_____
_____
_____
_____
_____
_____
_____
_____
_____

Comprehensive Problem for Part 4

Analyzing a Company for its Investment Potential

AltaGas Ltd., a Canadian energy infrastructure company, included a five-year summary of its operating and financial record highlights on its website (www.altagas.ca). Selected information is shown below.

Required

Analyze the company's Financial Highlights for the fiscal years 2009 to 2013. Include the following sections in your analysis and explain if you think this business is doing well or not:

- Trend analysis (use 2009 as the base year): Analyses for net revenue, net income, total assets, and shareholders' equity are suggested.
- Profitability analysis: Returns on sales, return on equity, and earnings per share would be key.

($ millions except per-share amounts) Income Statement[1]	2013	2012	2011	2010	2009
Net Revenue[2]	960.2	664.4	513.1	504.8	456.6
EBITDA[2]	538.9	319.4	257.2	234.9	251.5
EBITDA per basic share	$4.64	$3.36	$3.06	$2.88	$3.20
Operating income[2]	360.1	214.1	175.1	152.1	174.3
Net income	181.5	101.8	82.7	117.0	141.3
Net income per basic share	$1.56	$1.07	$0.98	$1.43	$1.80
Dividends declared per share	$1.50	$1.40	$1.34	$0.66	
Balance Sheet					
Capital assets	4,952.5	3,949.2	2,486.1	1,923.50	1,857.1
Intangible assets	195.3	189.8	177.5	80.0	128.9
Total assets	7,281.3	5,932.4	3,556.2	2,743.10	2,628.90
Short-term debt	84.4	66.9	16.8	9.5	14.5
Long-term debt	2,925.7	2,626.1	1,214.3	903.0	1,000.10
Shareholders' equity	2,791.7	1,959.8	1,355.4	1,209.90	1,048.90
Ratios (percent)					
Return on average equity	9.4	7.8	8.0	9.44	13.6
Return on average invested capital	8.5	7.7	8.5	8.23	10.0

Notes:

(1) Columns may not add due to rounding.

(2) Non-GAAP financial measure. See discussion in previous public disclosures available on this website or our SEDAR profile page.

	2013	2012	2011	2010	2009
Trend Analysis:					
Net revenue					
Net income					
Total assets					
Shareholders' equity					
Profitability Measures:					
Return on sales					
Return on equity					
Earnings per share					

Calculations: